S0-BSM-108

Women's Rights

Look for these and other books in the Lucent Overview Series:

Abortion
Adoption
Advertising
Alcoholism
Cancer
Child Abuse
Children's Rights
Drug Abuse
Drugs and Sports
Eating Disorders
Euthanasia
Family Violence
Gangs
Gay Rights
Homeless Children
Homelessness
Illegal Immigration
Illiteracy
Juvenile Crime
Mental Illness
Population
Poverty
Prisons
Recycling
Schools
Smoking
Sports in America
Suicide
Teen Alcoholism
Teen Pregnancy
Teen Sexuality
Teen Suicide
Women's Rights
World Hunger

Women's Rights

by Wendy Mass

For my sisters, Allison and Jennifer,
and pacts made on ferries.

Library of Congress Cataloging-in-Publication Data

Mass, Wendy, 1967–
Women's rights / Wendy Mass.
p. cm. — (Lucent overview series)
Includes bibliographical references and index.
ISBN 1-56006-510-9 (alk. paper)
1. Women's rights—United States—History. 2. Women—Suffrage—United States—History. 3. Feminism—United States—History. I. Title. II. Series.
HQ1236.5.U6M3779 1998
305.42'0973—dc21 97-29945
CIP
AC

P.O. Box 289011, San Diego, CA 92198-9011
Printed in the U.S.A.

Contents

INTRODUCTION	6
CHAPTER ONE Women Fight for the Right to Vote: The Suffrage Movement	8
CHAPTER TWO Equality in Education	18
CHAPTER THREE Equality in the Workplace	28
CHAPTER FOUR Violence Against Women	46
CHAPTER FIVE Reproductive Rights	59
CHAPTER SIX The Plight of Women Around the Globe	69
NOTES	80
ORGANIZATIONS TO CONTACT	84
SUGGESTIONS FOR FURTHER READING	87
WORKS CONSULTED	89
INDEX	92
ABOUT THE AUTHOR	96
PICTURE CREDITS	96

Introduction

Among the many important questions which have been brought before the public, there is none that more vitally affects the whole human family than that which is technically called Women's Rights.

—Elizabeth Cady Stanton

THE DECLARATION OF INDEPENDENCE proclaimed that all men are equal and possess the rights to life, liberty, and the pursuit of happiness. For 220 years, American women have been trying to prove that they deserve the same. The foundation for women's inequality goes back thousands of years. In fact, according to the Bible, it goes back to the beginning of humankind. In the Book of Genesis, Eve tempts Adam into eating the forbidden fruit. As a punishment, God says, "I will greatly multiply your pain in childbirth; in pain you shall bring forth children, yet your desire shall be for your husband, *and he shall rule over you*" [emphasis added].

A hundred and fifty years ago, a handful of European and American women decided to change their second-class role in society, realizing that change depended on the power to vote alongside men. After nearly seventy years of fighting, women finally won that right in 1920.

Between 1920 and the 1960s, women fought (and won) another major battle for the right to purchase and use contraceptives. In the widespread social upheaval of the 1960s, the women's rights movement gained new prominence. Betty Friedan published *The Feminine Mystique* and influenced a

Suffragettes from different states make their way to Washington, D.C., in February 1913.

generation of women to confront the remaining inequalities between the sexes. The National Organization for Women (NOW) was formed and is still the largest feminist organization in America fighting to secure, through the creation of new laws or the abolishment of old ones, women's rights in the home, the workplace, the school system, on the streets of America, and throughout the world. Since 1923 women's rights groups wanted these goals to be sanctioned by a constitutional amendment called the Equal Rights Amendment (ERA), which would guarantee both sexes equal treatment under the law. The amendment has faced stiff opposition in light of much recent state and federal legislation protecting women's rights, however, and though the ERA was passed in Congress, it has never been ratified by the required majority of the states.

Although women have achieved many of their goals toward equality, those in the women's rights movement believe women have a long way to go, including changing some long-held perceptions about the traditional roles of men and women. According to Gloria Steinem, the outspoken journalist, founder of *MS.* magazine, and crusader for women's rights, "Women can't be equal *outside* of the home until men are equal *inside* the home."[1]

1

Women Fight for the Right to Vote: The Suffrage Movement

AS FAMED ANTHROPOLOGIST Margaret Mead once said, "Never doubt that a small group of thoughtful, committed citizens can change the world; indeed it's the only thing that ever has." In the mid-1800s, just such a group was formed by a handful of women dedicated to securing for women the right to vote. They knew that a campaign for other human rights would be doomed unless women were able to cast their vote for the people they wanted to represent them in government. Without that power, all women could do was beg for change while men voted against their wishes time and time again. It took over seventy years of determination and constant campaigning to win the vote, finally securing women the freedom to have their voices heard and counted.

A woman's place

The fight for the right to vote, known as the suffrage movement, began around 1840. Women held a very specific place in society at that time. They were expected to marry, raise a family, and take care of a household. Although few, mostly poor, women worked outside the home, they were often not allowed to keep their wages (their salaries went either to their fathers or their husbands if they were married) and women usually relinquished custody of their children in the rare instance of divorce. Most women had no access to education higher than the primary level, and most could neither buy nor sell property. Women could not vote on issues that affected their families' lives, nor could they sit on juries, defend themselves in court, or run for political office.

Women were, in effect, considered the property of men. In a country that fifty years earlier had adopted a democratic Constitution, women—who accounted for half of the population—were basically rendered powerless.

"Power over themselves"

In 1792, British author Mary Wollstonecraft published an essay that condemned the conventions of her day. Wollstonecraft was one of the first women to speak out about the inequality between men and women. In *A Vindication of the Rights of Woman*, she assures her readers that as an activist for women's rights, she wants women to have power not over men, but over themselves. She argues that men and women are intellectual equals, and that male authors and journalists are responsible for the false idea that women are "artificial, weak characters . . . and useless members of society."[2] The essay gained a limited readership in England, but not until well into the next century did its message attract widespread attention among American women. It prompted the first rumblings of discontent as women determined that there was something seriously wrong with how they were treated in society.

With the publication of her 1792 essay, Mary Wollstonecraft publicly challenged society's treatment of women.

By the time John Stuart Mill's book *The Subjection of Women* was published in 1869, the seeds of the women's movement had already been planted. Mill's book was a heartfelt, philosophical plea for perfect equality. He believed the book gained widespread recognition among both sexes and lent further credence to the fact that women had practically no rights when compared to men. Wollstonecraft's book laid the foundation for the women's movement; Mill's book gave it legitimacy. Together, these works helped inspire a few key women who decided it was time to let their voices be heard.

The abolitionist movement

Yet women did not organize on a large scale to fight for their rights, at first. The fight to end slavery, called the abolitionist movement, was the first issue to band women together for a common cause. Often, the fight to free the slaves and the fight for women's rights were linked. While William Lloyd Garrison, founder of the American Anti-Slavery Society, argued for the rights of slaves, he also spoke out for women's rights, and women paid attention. Many women opposed slavery on moral or religious grounds, and even felt a kinship with the plight of the slaves. They offered their support to the abolitionists, but few abolitionist organizations admitted women members, so a young woman named Lucretia Mott formed the Philadelphia Female Anti-Slavery Society. Women in other cities followed suit: Women learned how to organize a political campaign, print pamphlets, conduct meetings, create petitions, and, perhaps most importantly for their future work as suffragists, make the most of opportunities to lecture in public. Before the days of television or radio, most people attended lectures to hear opinions on local and world issues. Though at first women were allowed to lecture only to other women in small groups, women such as reformers Angelina Grimké and her sister Sarah managed to break through the barrier. Angelina preached her message to anyone who would listen, and her brilliance as a speaker began to attract men as

Lucretia Mott, shown here at a much older age than when she fought for suffrage. When abolitionist groups refused to admit her and other women as members, she formed her own organization.

Sarah Grimké (pictured) and her sister Angelina worked tirelessly for women's equality and the abolitionist cause.

well as women to her lectures. Sarah was the writer in the family, and, in a letter, requested of men "that they take their feet from off our necks and permit us to stand upright on that ground which God designed us to occupy."[3] In 1838 Angelina became the first woman to address a legislative body in the United States when she presented the New York legislature with antislavery petitions signed by twenty thousand women. This small victory sent out an important message—that women's opinions should be considered by lawmakers. Yet, when the World Anti-Slavery Convention was held in London two years later, women were still not allowed to participate. This insult was lucky, however, as it led to the meeting of two of the most influential women in American history, Lucretia Mott and Elizabeth Cady Stanton. Informed that they were not going to be allowed to participate at the convention, they wandered the streets of London together and vowed to change the plight of women. Not until eight years later were they able to put their plan into action.

Organizing a revolt

Elizabeth Cady Stanton lived in the small farming town of Seneca Falls, New York. It was there that she and Lucretia Mott decided to hold the first Women's Rights Convention in 1848. Well educated and fervently dedicated to improving life for women, Stanton became known as the "Mother of the Suffrage Movement." Using the Declaration of Independence as a model, she composed the Seneca Falls Declaration of Sentiments and Resolutions. The lengthy document began with nearly identical wording: "We hold these truths to be self-evident: that all men and women are created equal; that they are endowed by their Creator with certain inalienable rights." Then, Stanton

added, "The history of mankind is a history of repeated injuries and usurpations on the part of man toward woman, having in direct object the establishment of an absolute tyranny over her."[4] She listed the areas in which women should demand equality, and shocked everyone by including the right to vote.

Frederick Douglass, a well-known abolitionist and former slave, strongly supported her position. The strength of his conviction and prestige encouraged the members of the convention to sign the declaration and agree to fight for suffrage. This decision set off a huge wave of opposition; Stanton soon discovered that

Elizabeth Cady Stanton organized the first Women's Rights Convention in the town of Seneca Falls, New York, in 1848.

> all the journals, from Maine to Texas, seemed to strive with each other to see which could make our movement appear the most ridiculous. . . . So pronounced was the popular voice against us, in the parlor, press, and pulpit, that most of the ladies who had attended the convention and signed the declaration, one by one, withdrew their names and influences.[5]

A local newspaper called the whole convention the most shocking and unnatural incident ever recorded in the history of humanity. The suffragists were called "men haters" and "old maids" and told that women were too emotional to reach fair political decisions. Critics claimed that women would base their decisions on which candidate was more attractive rather than who was the best qualified.

Not to be held back by these harsh criticisms, Mott and Stanton continued speaking out at conventions springing up around the country, joined eventually by two women who would turn out to be important leaders, Susan B. Anthony and Lucy Stone. During the next ten years the suffragists campaigned relentlessly, facing opposition everywhere they spoke.

While the suffragists battled the opposition, the Civil War broke out between the North and the South. Many of the men who had previously supported the suffragists asked them to set aside their own goals and focus their work on helping to free the slaves.

Civil War

Women did put aside the suffrage issue as they directed their energies toward the war effort. Women on both sides of the conflict helped make ammunition and worked as nurses. In the North, Stanton and Anthony formed the Women's National Loyalty League, which campaigned to end slavery, calculating that the federal government would grant the right to vote to women as well as freed slaves. In 1865, at the end of the war, the Thirteenth Amendment prohibited slavery or the denial of other liberties "without due process of law." A large civil rights bill (which would become the Fourteenth Amendment) was also proposed, granting broad rights to all slaves as well as other citizens. The amendment was supposed to make all former slaves U.S. citizens, thereby entitled to the right to vote. Women were thrilled, because they assumed this meant that they, too, would finally get the right to vote. They were wrong. The Fourteenth Amendment clearly stated that the right to vote was extended to black males only, not to females, black or white. These acts of Congress infuriated the suffragists and, in 1869, caused a split within their ranks. Although both factions still fought for suffrage, their emphasis was different. Stanton and Anthony formed the National Woman Suffrage Association and devoted themselves to achieving the vote at the federal level. They urged Congress to support a new constitutional amendment which would read, "The right of citizens of the United States to vote, shall not be denied or abridged by the United States or by any state on account of sex." Meanwhile, Lucy Stone formed the American Woman Suffrage Association, which focused on getting the states to individually grant women the right to vote. The two groups worked independently; each made slow progress.

Women continued to be prominent in political efforts that they felt had an impact on women, including the

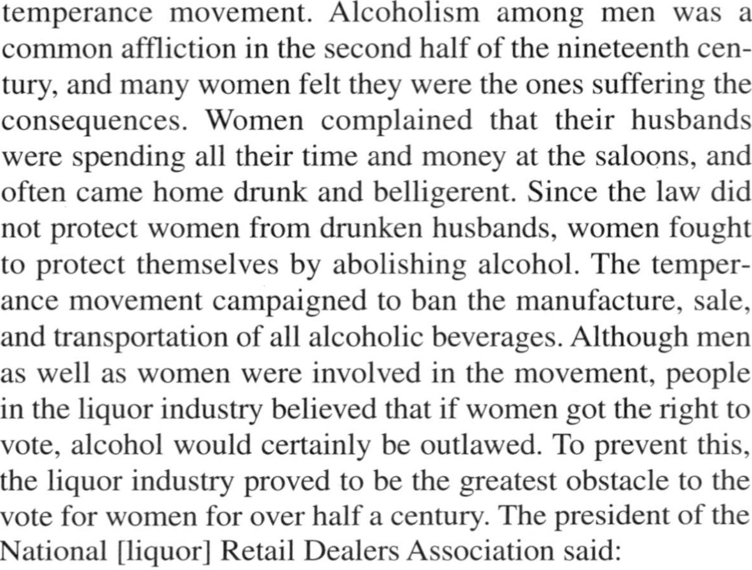

temperance movement. Alcoholism among men was a common affliction in the second half of the nineteenth century, and many women felt they were the ones suffering the consequences. Women complained that their husbands were spending all their time and money at the saloons, and often came home drunk and belligerent. Since the law did not protect women from drunken husbands, women fought to protect themselves by abolishing alcohol. The temperance movement campaigned to ban the manufacture, sale, and transportation of all alcoholic beverages. Although men as well as women were involved in the movement, people in the liquor industry believed that if women got the right to vote, alcohol would certainly be outlawed. To prevent this, the liquor industry proved to be the greatest obstacle to the vote for women for over half a century. The president of the National [liquor] Retail Dealers Association said:

Susan B. Anthony (left) and Elizabeth Cady Stanton (right) worked to end slavery in the hope that, when Congress freed the slaves and gave them the right to vote, women's suffrage would also be included in the legislation.

> We need not fear the churches, the men are voting the old tickets; we need not fear the ministers, for the most part they follow the men of the churches; we need not fear the Y.M.C.A., for it does not do aggressive work, but, gentlemen, we need to fear the Woman's Christian Temperance Union and the ballot in the hands of women; therefore, gentlemen, fight woman suffrage![6]

The liquor lobby fought the suffrage movement both publicly—by running ads and raising money to oppose it—and indirectly, with threats and bribery of state officials. Liquor companies made political campaign contributions to politicians in exchange for their promise to vote against suffrage. The liquor lobby was credited as a real force in successfully holding off suffrage in state elections across the country, but one by one, suffragists were gaining ground.

In 1869 the territory of Wyoming gave women the right to vote. Women were also granted the right to sit on juries. The women in the territory quickly earned a reputation for being thorough and strict and not afraid to impose punishments on criminals. When Wyoming was officially admitted to the Union in 1890, it brought the women's right to vote with it, making it the first state to grant suffrage to women. Three years later, Colorado passed a similar law, followed by both Utah (where women had been voting since 1870, when Utah was still a territory) and Idaho in 1896.

A nineteenth-century illustration depicts armored women leading the fight to abolish alcohol. The liquor lobby fought against the suffrage movement, fearing that if women were allowed to vote, they would vote to make alcohol illegal.

The two women's suffrage groups reunited in 1890, calling themselves the National American Woman Suffrage Association and continuing to rally for women's rights. By the early 1900s, a new generation of suffragists, led by Carrie Chapman Catt and Alice Paul, headed up the National American Woman Suffrage Association. Alice Paul broke away from the association and formed the Congressional Union for Woman Suffrage (later known as the National Women's Party), a more radical and militant group that picketed the White House and held hunger strikes. By 1917 sixteen states had granted women the vote, but the federal government still held out. At that point, though, women's voting power did contribute greatly to the passing of the Eighteenth Amendment banning the manufacturing and selling of alcohol and ushering in the era of Prohibition.

The Nineteenth Amendment

In 1918 President Woodrow Wilson agreed to support an amendment allowing women to vote. The wording of the proposed amendment was unchanged since Susan B. Anthony wrote it in 1878. With the support of the president, the amendment passed in the House of Representatives, and a year and a half later, passed in the Senate by two votes. The amendment then had to be ratified by two-thirds, or thirty-two, of the forty-eight states. By March 1920, thirty-five states had voted to ratify it, eight had defeated it, and only five states remained to decide the issue. The only state legislature that was even considering ratification was Tennessee's. The nation's attention was focused on this state, which was deeply divided. After emotional campaigning on both sides, the Tennessee House of Representatives took its vote. Everyone expected a tie: forty-eight men were known to support the amendment and forty-eight publicly opposed it. But twenty-four-year-old opponent Harry Burn changed his vote, claiming he had promised his mother that in the event of a tie, he would vote for the amendment. He said, "I appreciated the fact that an opportunity such as seldom comes to a mortal man to free seventeen million women from political slavery was mine."[7] The number was actually closer to 25 million. When the Nineteenth Amendment to the Constitution became law on August 26, 1920, Carrie Chapman Catt established the League of Women Voters, an organization dedicated to educating the huge new voting bloc on the political issues of the day. Women had a lot of catching up to do in the world of politics, and often had to be encouraged to use their newfound influence at the polls.

Alice Paul formed a radical and militant suffrage group that picketed the White House and held hunger strikes to protest Congress's lack of action on women's suffrage.

The legacy

In the presidential elections of 1980 women voters outnumbered men for the first time, setting a new precedent for women's political power. Senator Dianne Feinstein of California believes that since 1980, women have been de-

Women in U.S. Cabinet-Level Positions
(As of April 1997)

Administration	Total Appointees	Total Women	Percent Women
Carter (1977–1981)	21	3	14.3
Reagan (1981–1989)	28	5	17.9
Bush (1989–1993)	17	6	35.3
Clinton (1993–1997)	22	9	40.9

termining elections. Senator Olympia Snowe of Maine points out: "From the classroom to the workroom, the legislative changes pushed by women will touch the lives of most every woman and her family through expanded medical research on women's health, better protection against domestic violence, and improved social opportunities."[8] And Senator Kay Bailey Hutchison of Texas sums up the impact of the suffrage movement: "When you look at the issues we tackle in Congress today that affect women, you just have to appreciate that none of this would have happened unless we had the right to vote."[9] Susan B. Anthony's battle cry, "Failure Is Impossible," has kept women fighting for their rights for over 150 years.

2
Equality in Education

WITH FEW EXCEPTIONS, most American universities and graduate schools today enroll equal numbers of women and men. In some cases women slightly outnumber men. Women now have access to the same programs of study as men, and can pursue the same careers upon graduation. Only a century ago, however, most American women were denied higher education. Middle-class white women were raised to expect a life geared toward managing a home and family, where a higher education would be useless. Many people of the time argued that it must even be detrimental, encouraging women to abandon hearth and home. As in the fight for suffrage, some women and men fought for women's right to higher education.

Why bother?

Most girls stopped attending school after elementary school. Usually around age ten, a girl would be taken out of school to begin work at her mother's side while her brothers often continued in school—even going on to college. If a family decided to allow a daughter to continue her education, it was usually done through a private tutor.

Many people began to view the denial of higher education to women as unfair. Denied the right to vote, as well, women had to plead their case to whomever would listen. The first man to speak out on the subject of women's education was physician and professor Benjamin Rush of

Philadelphia. A signer of the Declaration of Independence, Rush said that "women in a democratic republic ought to be qualified to a certain degree by a peculiar and suitable education" so that they could teach their sons "the principles of liberty and government."[10] Rush's comment was taken as backhanded by some women because it intimated that only a woman's sons, not the woman or her daughters, would benefit from a mother's education.

Milestones in education

In 1819, Emma Willard, the wife of a headmaster of a boys' school, petitioned the New York State legislature for the money to start a school for women. She was turned down but managed to raise the money on her own. In 1821 the Troy Female Seminary opened as the first college for women. One of its first graduates was Elizabeth Cady (Stanton), who would go on to play a huge role in the fight for women's voting rights.

Benjamin Rush supported women's education but only as a means of qualifying women to teach their sons "the principles of liberty and government."

In 1834, a year after its founding, Oberlin College in Ohio became the first in the country to allow women to attend; the administration thought that the presence of women would have a calming effect on their rowdy male students. At first young women were allowed to take only classes that would prepare them to be proper wives. They were also obliged to wash the male students' clothes, clean their rooms, and serve them dinner, and they were not allowed to speak publicly. In 1837, Mt. Holyoke opened in Massachusetts as the first women's college to offer a full range of courses leading to the bachelor of arts degree. Historian Eleanor Flexner writes: "The way had been cleared for the opening of Vassar in 1865, of Smith and Wellesley in 1875, of the 'Harvard Annex' (Radcliffe) in 1879 and of Bryn Mawr in 1885. It was becoming clear, to the dismay and regret of some, that there was no telling where it would end."[11]

Well into the 1960s, although they had much better access to universities, women students were still not treated the same as men. At Harvard women were denied access to the best library and banned from the freshmen dining room. Few schools offered comparable college-level sports programs for women; some set their admission standards at a higher level for girls than boys. In the 1970s, Congress began passing laws protecting women against discrimination in academia.

The formation of Title IX

In 1972, Congress passed the Educational Amendments Act, a comprehensive set of regulations addressing the issue of gender inequality in education. The foundation of the act was Title IX, which states that "no person in the United States shall, on the basis of sex, be excluded from participation in, be denied the benefits of, or be subjected to discrimination under any education program or activity receiving Federal financial assistance." The law did not affect the admission policies of single-sex elementary and secondary schools, private undergraduate schools, or public undergraduate schools "that traditionally and continually" admitted students of one sex. The statute also excluded military academies and religious schools. Two years later, Congress amended the statute to exclude fraternities, sororities, the YMCA and YWCA, Boy Scouts, Girls Scouts, and Campfire Girls. With the help of the Education Task Force—composed of organizations like the National Student Lobby, the Project on the Status and Education of Women, and the Project on Equal Education Rights—the federal government continued to more clearly define and expand the rights under Title IX protection. By 1979, the provision had been expanded to allow women to sue discriminatory schools, call for "equal athletic opportunity for members of both sexes," and require schools to provide an equal number of athletic scholarships to men and women. By guaranteeing these rights, Title IX has allowed many women the opportunity to fight injustices in court.

Title IX fights for its life

In 1984 the Supreme Court severely restricted the scope of Title IX by ruling that a school was not subject to the antidiscrimination requirements of Title IX if the particular school program or activity in question was not directly receiving federal aid. This halted hundreds of discrimination cases pending before the Department of Education and greatly angered legislators, women's rights groups, and the civil rights community who interpreted the ruling as a green light for schools to revert back to past discriminatory practices. Congress immediately set out to draw up legislation that would reverse the Supreme Court's decision, but it took four years before the bill, called the Civil Rights Restoration Act, passed both the House of Representatives and the Senate. President Ronald Reagan then vetoed the bill after its 1988 passage, saying it gave the government too much power over the affairs and decisions of private institutions.

Less than a week later, on March 22, 1988, Congress voted to override Reagan's veto and the Civil Rights Restoration Act became law. The act not only restored the rights guaranteed under Title IX, but extended them to cover many more aspects of discrimination within the educational arena.

Equal Educational Opportunities Act

In 1974, not long after Title IX was originally enacted, Congress had passed the Equal Educational Opportunities Act, which declared that "all children enrolled in public schools are entitled to equal educational opportunity without regard to race, color, sex, or national origin." This law made it easier to break the barriers girls faced when they wanted to, for example, take wood shop instead of cooking, and gave boys the same freedom of choice. School guidance counselors were informed they could not steer girls exclusively towards traditional fields for women, such as teaching and nursing, and ordered to cease giving male or female students gender-specific aptitude or vocational tests, which skewed results by not allowing a fair comparison between the sexes. Practices like these can be hard to detect, however, and may still be continuing in schools today.

Progress is also being made at the state level. For example, California legislation requires schools to use instructional materials that portray the contributions of women in all fields and forbids the use of materials that depict women as inferior. Other states are expected to adopt similar legislation.

All-male admission policy declared unconstitutional

In 1990 the attorney general of Virginia challenged the right of the all-male Virginia Military Institute (VMI) to exclude women under Title IV of the 1964 Civil Rights Act. The attorney general claimed that VMI supporters practiced sexual discrimination. VMI replied that the presence of women would disrupt its extraordinarily demanding physical and mental regimen and "destroy the institution in its current form." The case was batted back and forth in the courts without a solution. Meanwhile, in 1993, high-school student Shannon Faulkner applied to the all-male Citadel, a 155-year-old rigorous military academy in South Carolina. She was accepted because the admissions board thought she was male. Once the error was detected, the school refused to admit her. After a battle waged in

court and in the media she was finally admitted to the full program in the fall of 1995. She wound up leaving the school soon after she began due to stress and her inability to perform the arduous physical regimen, but she had set a precedent that the Supreme Court finally acknowledged.

In 1996, in a 7 to 1 Supreme Court vote, the all-male admission policy of state-supported schools like VMI and the Citadel was declared unconstitutional. The only dissenting voice was that of Justice Antonin Scalia. (Justice Clarence Thomas abstained because his son attended VMI.) Justice Ruth Bader Ginsburg wrote the majority opinion that the exclusion of women from the military schools' educational opportunities denied them equal protection guaranteed by the U.S. Constitution: "However well this plan serves the state's sons, it makes no provision whatever for her daughters."[12] The Court claimed that VMI's objection to coeducation reflected the same ancient fear that had long kept women out of the field of law and other professions. VMI

Shannon Faulkner greets the dean of the Citadel before attending her first class on January 20, 1994. Faulkner left the school soon after, unable to cope with the vigorous physical regimen recruits received.

opened its enrollment to women in August 1997, and four young women entered the Citadel in August 1996. Their first year there showed both schools that coeducation will be a bumpy road.

The results of coeducation at the Citadel

Three of the women who enrolled in the Citadel's first coed class in 1996 had family ties to the school and a long history of military involvement. When the fourth female student announced financial trouble, a group of alumni banded together in a show of support to pay her tuition. According to the regimental commander of the corps of cadets, "not one male incoming freshman I've talked to said he didn't want to attend because women would be here."[13] This initial goodwill was apparently limited, however; after two months in school, two of the women, citing the sexual harassment and hazing they received from many of the male cadets, did not return for the second semester. One of the two claimed that male cadets routinely entered her bedroom in the middle of the night and "repeatedly made sexual comments about me in my spandex [sleepwear] shorts."[14] The young men are also accused of setting fire to the clothes one girl was wearing, barging in when the women had just come out of the shower, and forcing them to stand in metal cabinets while being punched and kicked. The two other young women successfully completed their first year without incident.

In response to the allegations of harassment, the Citadel disciplined at least fourteen male cadets, with punishments ranging from expulsion to marching in the barracks courtyard and campus confinement. The FBI and the State Law

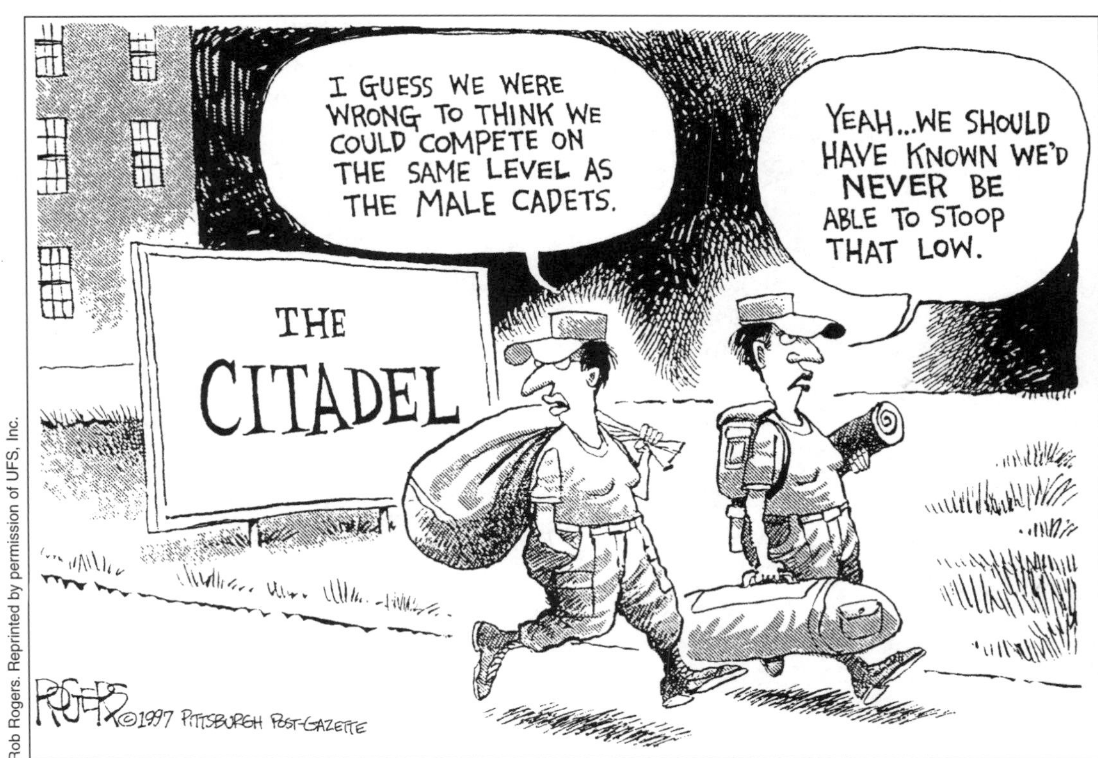

Enforcement Division are further investigating the women's claims. An ad hoc committee comprising former Citadel officers, community leaders, and a female graduate of the U.S. Air Force Academy reported its conviction that in many areas the college does not fully comprehend the implications of and responsibilities it faces as a coeducational military college. The committee also faulted the Citadel for its public stance against accepting women in the first place. The administration and public relations departments of both schools are working hard to ensure a welcoming atmosphere so that future female students will not face the animosity faced by those of the class of 1996.

Women teachers and professors struggle for equality

Currently the majority of primary and secondary schoolteachers are women (72 percent); however, the majority of school principals and headmasters (71 percent) are men. The American Association of University Professors reports that in the mid-1990s women hold only 22.6 percent of tenured positions on college faculties, with many esteemed schools falling below that range. In 1970, after the Women's Equity Action League filed complaints of sex discrimination against three hundred universities, schools were threatened with the loss of federal funds until they began to hire and promote more women. But today the courts are still filled with these suits, and statistics regarding female tenure are perceived by some women as proof of ongoing discrimination. Just 13 percent of the tenured positions at Columbia University and Stanford are filled by women; 12 percent at Princeton, just over 11 percent at Harvard, 10 percent at the University of Michigan, and 9.4 percent at Yale. Joseph McCarthy, assistant dean of academic planning for the faculty of arts and sciences at Harvard, argues that women who reach the top of their profession often turn down positions because they are unwilling to relocate and uproot their families, and maintains that as more women enter academia, the relatively small number of women at the top of their fields will increase, thus increasing the number of female professors that Harvard would be interested in hiring. But the Committee for the Equality of Women at Harvard conducted a thorough exploration of the history of women in higher education and found that "university officials exaggerate claims that too few women Ph.Ds exist, and that if there is a shortfall, the universities themselves bear the blame for not recruiting and supporting women students."[15]

Today women in education have a number of laws to protect them against sex discrimination. In 1982 the Supreme Court ended a long controversy about the rights granted to women in education by Title IX. The Court decided that the law does in fact protect employees in federally funded education programs from discrimination on the basis of sex, thereby covering teachers, administrators, and other school employees. In addition to Title IX, teachers are rallying against sexual discrimination by claiming the protection guaranteed by Titles IV and VII of the 1964 Civil Rights Act, the Equal Pay Act, and the Equal Protection Clause if they are public school employees. Academia is only one area of the workforce where women have fought to secure equality. Women over the centuries have also faced obstacles in the way of career advancement, and in the past few decades, the laws are finally beginning to protect them.

3

Equality in the Workplace

TODAY, SEVEN OUT of every ten women in America are employed full-time. The struggle for equality with men in the workplace, however, is still being waged against such issues as discrimination in hiring practices, wage disparity, hindered advancement, and sexual harassment. Working mothers have additional concerns, including maternity leave, day care, or limited chances for advancement if their careers are interrupted by periods of child rearing. Many women who are trying to balance their careers and their home life find they must make compromises to handle both. The past few decades have provided women with laws to protect them against workplace discrimination, and most employers are making a concerted effort to address the concerns of female employees.

Women enter the workforce

In the early 1900s, most of the women who worked out of the home worked in other people's homes as cooks, maids, and laundresses. Women could also be farm laborers, nurses, salesclerks, and teachers, or they could work from their home by taking in laundry, rolling cigarettes, or sewing clothes by the piece. With the invention of the typewriter and other office machines, women began working in offices as bookkeepers, stenographers, or secretaries, but without the possibility of promotion. The workers in garment factories were almost exclusively women and chil-

dren who were paid according to how many pieces of clothing they completed. Women worked up to twelve hours a day, and if they started working too efficiently, an employer was likely to lower the amount of money paid for each garment. The factories of early industrialized American cities were known as sweatshops because they were usually overcrowded, dimly lit, smelly, and very hot. But opportunities for women were so few, especially for new immigrants, that many had no choice but to continue working under oppressive or unsafe conditions.

Women work in a textile and garment factory. When women were able to increase their piece rate, managers often lowered their salary in order to keep wages down.

When America entered World War I, the workplace changed for women. They were now needed to fill the places of the men who were sent to fight and to contribute their labor to the war effort. They took over jobs previously closed to them, and the U.S. Department of Labor created the Women in Industry Service to monitor women's working conditions. During the war, women accounted for more than 20 percent of the workers who manufactured airplanes and other machinery, food, printed materials, and leather and rubber goods. They were hired by the thousands for government clerical services, and over one hundred thousand women worked on the railroads. Women's salaries were considerably higher than those paid by their more traditional jobs before the war, but they were rarely the same as men's.

When the war ended, most of the women were forced out of their new skilled labor positions and back into fields like food preparation and garment manufacturing.

Women in politics bring reforms

During the depression of the 1930s, most working women lost their jobs. Eleanor Roosevelt used her position as First Lady to help women gain more rights in the workplace. She encouraged her husband, President Franklin D. Roosevelt, to appoint more women to government positions and helped call attention to the inequities of women in the workplace, both employed and recently unemployed. Frances Perkins became the first woman cabinet member when Roosevelt appointed her secretary of labor. She supported a minimum wage, maximum work hours,

Eleanor Roosevelt (right) and Mary McLeod Bethune (left) at a conference in 1939. Roosevelt made sure that African Americans and women were hired for positions during her husband's administration.

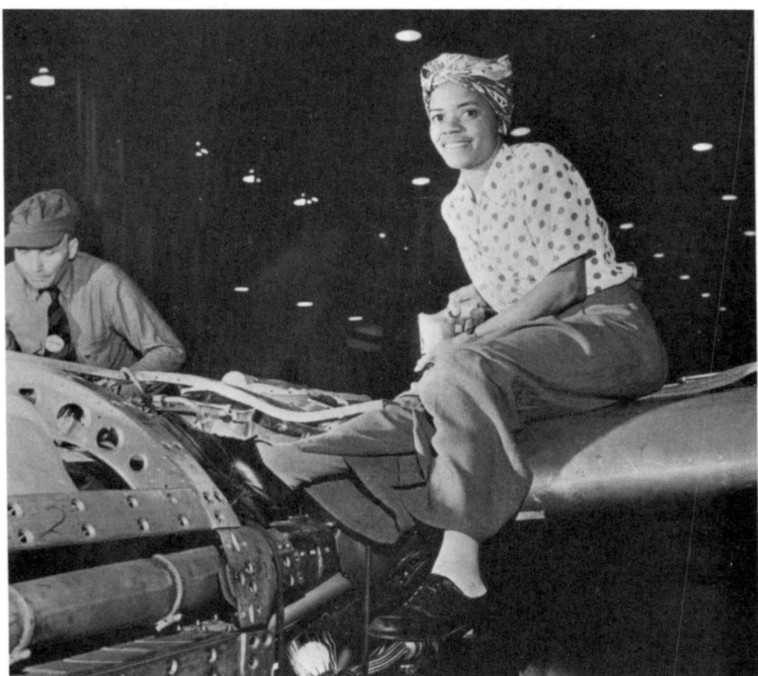

A female riveter works on aircraft during World War II. During the war, millions of women entered the workforce.

and an end to child labor. Ruth Bryan Owen was named ambassador to Denmark, thereby becoming the first woman diplomat. Roosevelt also made great strides for African American women by naming Mary McLeod Bethune as the Negro Affairs Director for the National Youth Administration. She was instrumental in helping thousands of women get jobs and scholarships to college.

With the onset of World War II, women once again entered the workforce in the millions. And once again, when the war ended they were forced back out to be wives and mothers. Until the women's rights movements of the 1960s, women were primarily stuck in low-paying and undervalued jobs, without access to professional positions. By the '60s, the culture of America was changing. Not every woman wanted to be a wife and mother, but women who tried to pursue a career found most doors closed to them. Some outspoken women finally decided they were tired of being discriminated against and began demanding equal access to employment opportunities.

In 1964 the doors swung open with Title VII of the Civil Rights Act. This is the strongest piece of federal legislation protecting women's rights against discrimination in the workplace. Originally, the act was created to alleviate racial and minority discrimination in society, with Title VII focusing on employment issues. Amid much controversy within its ranks Congress decided to include sexual discrimination under the terms of Title VII, giving women the legal ammunition they needed to safeguard their rights in the workplace.

Equal employment opportunities

Title VII states that it is illegal for any employer "to fail or refuse to hire or to discharge any individual, or otherwise to discriminate against any individual with respect to his compensation, terms, conditions, or privileges of employment, because of such an individual's race, color, religion, sex, or national origin." An employer must not "limit, segregate, or classify his employees or applicants for employment in any way which would deprive or tend to deprive any individual of employment opportunities, or otherwise adversely affect his status as an employee, because of such an individual's race, color, religion, sex, or national origin." Newspapers and employment agencies were no longer allowed to advertise certain jobs only to particular sexes, thereby putting an end to deep-rooted job stereotyping. Initially the legislation applied only to companies or labor unions with more than twenty-five employees, but the Equal Employment Opportunity (EEO) Act of 1972 brought the minimum number down to fifteen.

But more than thirty years after Title VII, businesses still discriminate in hiring on the basis of sex. For instance, gun manufacturer Smith & Wesson refused to hire even one of the sixteen hundred women who applied for jobs in the company's factories over a two-year period. Government pressure finally forced the company, in 1995, to pay a $450,000 settlement to unfairly slighted applicants. The only exception to the law prohibiting employers from hiring one sex over the other is when the job is a bona fide occupational qualification (BFOQ) absolutely necessary to the running of the business. This includes positions like restaurant restroom attendants, in which case modesty and the patrons' comfort require hiring one sex over the other. Acting roles and modeling jobs are also considered BFOQ. Under the act's guidelines, most other employers found it hard to argue that hiring only men in certain positions was a necessity to run their business and had no choice but to give women access into all areas.

Initially forty-three states had labor laws that prevented women from working in certain occupations or regulated the conditions of their jobs. Many of these restrictions had to do with working conditions considered harmful to women who may be pregnant, including exposure to potentially harmful chemicals and heavy lifting. Other jobs such as potentially dangerous night shifts, were given to men to protect women. Barbara Brown and the coauthors of *Women's Rights and the Law* argue that the laws had little to do with protecting women, however, insisting that the laws "were based on stereotypes about women's transient and secondary role in the labor market and their weak physical condition as well as on the desire of male workers to reduce competition for higher paying jobs."[16] Once Title VII was passed, however, not a single state labor law has been able to stand up to it. Women have proven that they would rather take their chances in less than ideal working environments than not have the choice.

Although women are granted the right to work in the same jobs as men, employers may still avoid hiring them. This obstacle prompted controversial legislation that is still debated today.

Affirmative action

In 1964, the year in which the Civil Rights Act was passed, President Lyndon Johnson signed Executive Order 11246 (first presented by President John F. Kennedy) in an effort to increase employment and educational opportunities for women and minorities. The term "affirmative action" was coined when the order mandated that employers of specified size who do business with the federal government or receive federal funds actively seek to include women and minorities when hiring for jobs. A prevailing concern is that affirmative action policies might actually be harmful to a woman hired because her company needs more women; her coworkers (and she herself) might then wonder if she really got the job based on merit. However, the wording of the document did not specify quotas that employers had to meet, nor did it suggest that they hire less qualified people in an attempt to increase the diversity of their workforce. Rather, it stated that companies and educational institutions needed to set up certain recruitment and outreach programs, offer grants and fellowships to encourage women to enter previously restricted fields, and do a certain amount of business with qualified woman-owned companies. The order contends that "goals may not be rigid and inflexible quotas which must be met, but must be targets reasonably attainable by means of applying every good faith effort to make all aspects of the entire affirmative action program work."[17]

A volatile issue

Since its inception, affirmative action has been a very volatile issue, with strong arguments for and against it. No one denies that under affirmative action women have been given access to many jobs that were previously closed to them. The Supreme Court has upheld affirmative action as a constitutional way to combat widespread inequity in the workforce on the grounds that a history of discrimination in the workplace warrants special measures to rectify it. But opponents believe that affirmative action is just another form of discrimination, that by giving preference to one group (women or minorities) employers are, in effect, discriminating against another (white males). Activists like Phyllis Schlafly agree: "One reason why affirmative action is wrong," she says, "is that the woman receiving the benefit is not the woman who was discriminated against. Nobody should be entitled to receive a remedy for an injury suffered by someone else."[18]

Supporters of affirmative action believe that without a dedicated and regulated effort on the part of employers,

sex-based and racial discrimination would remain indefinitely. Women would be forced to fight sex discrimination on a case-by-case basis through individual lawsuits, which would be, as one author put it, "like attempting to drain the ocean with a spoon."[19] Nevertheless, many believe the program has outlived its usefulness; that it opened the doors that needed to be opened, and is now doing more harm than good. In November 1996, the state of California was the first to ban affirmative action in state-sponsored programs by a ballot initiative vote of 54 percent to 46 percent even though women's rights groups campaigned vigorously against the ban. California governor Pete Wilson had previously gone on record against the policy, asserting that "even the architects of this system . . . never intended that it would last forever."[20] California's decision and the threat of other states following suit is viewed by many women's rights groups as a large step backwards for women's equality. According to Audrey Tayse Haynes, the head of Business and Professional Women/USA, "How can anyone say we don't need affirmative action anymore? There isn't a

Workers' rights leader Dolores Huerta speaks in support of affirmative action at the California state capitol in 1995. Many women support affirmative action because they believe it provides equal access to jobs.

single statistic that says women have achieved equality, in terms of money or power or opportunity. Not one."[21]

Gender wage discrepancy

Around the same time as the 1964 Civil Rights Act and affirmative action were set into motion, the Equal Pay Act (EPA) was also passed. It followed a study by the Commission on the Status of Women, which John F. Kennedy created in 1961. The commission, chaired by Eleanor Roosevelt, issued a report in 1963 that showed women faced discrimination in the workplace in many areas, including unequal pay. The EPA "marked the entrance of the federal government into the field of safeguarding the right of women to hold employment on the same basis as men."[22] It stipulated that employers must pay men and women equally for comparable work. Comparable jobs need not be identical; rather, two jobs would be comparable if their value to the business is equal and they require substantially equal skill, effort, responsibility, and working conditions. Under the EPA women can bring their employers to court directly, but since 1978 the Equal Employment Opportunity Commission (EEOC) is mostly responsible for filing suit. The EEOC will investigate a claim and will attempt to negotiate a settlement on the employee's behalf, keeping the person's identity confidential. According to a member of the appellate court that judged the first case under the EPA, "Congress intended the Act to overcome the age-old belief in women's inferiority and to eliminate the depressing effects on living standards of reduced wages for female workers and the economic and social consequences which flow from it."[23]

A narrowing gap

Studies that compared the income of women across the board to that of men found that at the time the EPA legislation was passed, women earned on average fifty-nine cents for every dollar a man earned. In 1986 women earned sixty-four cents for every dollar earned by men, an increase of only five cents in over twenty years. In 1997 the ratio had risen to seventy-two cents to the dollar, and the Rand Corporation projected a rise to seventy-four cents by the year 2000. The differential even among college graduates is considerable: women make seventy-six cents to the dollar. One must also consider the fields being compared. Eighty percent of women work in occupations that pay less than those dominated by men, so it makes sense that as a whole, women will earn less. For instance, "stock clerks, who are predominantly male, earn more than bank tellers, who are predominantly female. Registered nurses (mostly female) earn less than mail carriers (mostly male)."[24] Moreover, in 1990, more than one in four women who held an undergraduate or graduate degree earned that degree in education, while less than two in a hundred earned it in engineering. In contrast, less than one in ten men earned their degree in education while one in four earned it in engineering. "Market demand," according to researchers, "dictates that a degree in engineering is worth more than a degree in education."[25]

If the comparison is between women and men in the exact same job, with the exact same qualifications, the gap narrows but does not disappear. Studies show that women in this category under twenty earn 92 percent as much as their male counterparts, women twenty-one to twenty-four earn 85 percent, and women twenty-five to thirty-four earn 78 percent. According to the U.S. Civil Rights Commission, "The gaps that do still exist are likely due to the fewer continuous years women have been in the workforce, and that women who have never interrupted their careers for any reason now earn at least 98% as much as their male counterparts."[26]

The differential is particularly revealing when men enter traditionally female jobs and vice versa; studies show that men earn more than their female counterparts, while the opposite is true when women enter traditionally male jobs, even though the EPA forbids such practices. For instance, 74 percent of female professors at one branch of the University of California earn less than their male colleagues,

John Trever, for the *Albuquerque Journal*. Reprinted with permission.

even with the same qualifications and years of experience. Conversely, male registered nurses earn $1.04 to a female's dollar, male office workers $1.09, and male cashiers $1.17. Meanwhile, female truck drivers are paid on average seventy cents to the male truck driver's dollar, female lawyers earn seventy-four cents compared to their male colleagues' dollar, and female physicians earned fifty-four cents to the dollar even though in 1996 women made up 54 percent of students entering Yale Medical School.

In addition to the fight for an equal salary, many women complain that their job advancement is limited more than their male coworkers.

The glass ceiling

The hindrance of a woman's advancement or promotion by artificial boundaries is called "hitting the glass ceiling." Women's rights advocates say that pervasive stereotypes and discrimination against women keep them at lower job levels and prevents them from competing for the higher jobs on an equal basis with men. A 1992 survey revealed that out of 439 women who had advanced to executive levels, 93 percent had witnessed "the glass ceiling" at some point during their careers. Even though women today account for nearly half the workforce, they hold only between 3 and 5 percent of the senior management-level positions, and only compose 0.5 percent of the boards of directors of the top U.S. corporations. In the decade between 1982 and 1992, the number of top female executives in the country's largest one thousand companies only increased by 4.5 percent, but female vice presidents rose 9 percent, which shows that women are slowly moving up the ranks. Still, according to researchers, "if women continue to move into top business ranks at the current rate, the numbers of male and female senior managers will not be equal until the year 2470."[27]

There is a twofold argument against the existence of the glass ceiling. First, critics insist that women simply have not been in the workforce long enough to reach high-level positions. They assert that most top management positions

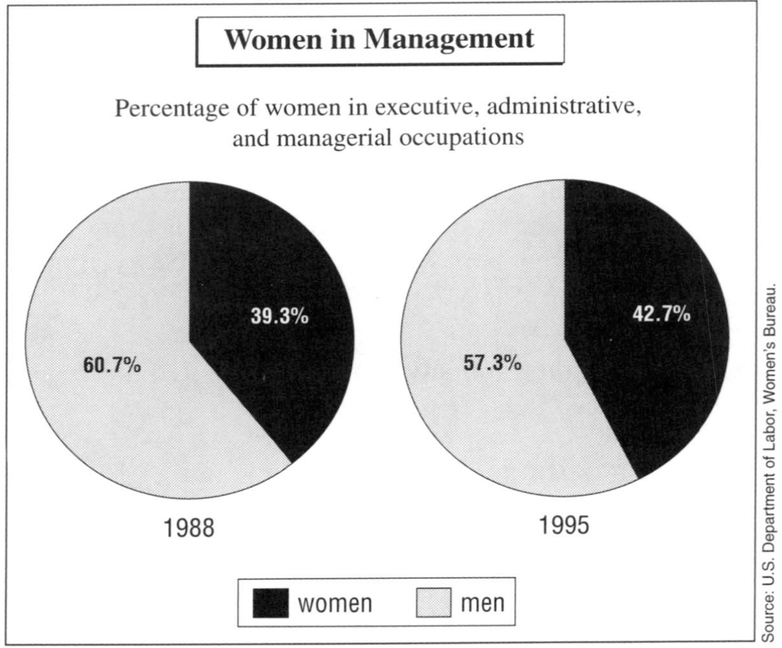

are filled by people who have been on the fast track for at least twenty-five years, which historically excludes most women. In the next decade or two, more women will reach that level of experience and the numbers of female CEOs and board members should increase accordingly. Secondly, promotions are based on continuous time in the workforce, and many more women than men take time off to raise children. A U.S. census report reveals that only 1.6 percent of a man's work years are spent away from work compared with 14.7 percent of a woman's. In the same vein, many women choose to remain in positions requiring less responsibility and time commitment so they can spend more time with their families. Only 55 percent of women who work full time work more than the required forty hours a week compared with 75 percent of men. The statistics, therefore, only show how many women work in high-level positions, not how many women actually want to be at those levels but cannot get there due to discriminatory practices.

Another measure of the situation is the thousands of cases brought to the Equal Employment Opportunity Commission each year. One woman who sued her employer was blatantly told she was not promoted because her company's clients felt more secure getting their advice from other men. The opposite reasoning was given to another woman who was turned down for partner at Price Waterhouse. She was told that the other partners would respond to her better if she learned to "walk more femininely, talk more femininely, dress more femininely, wear makeup, have her hair styled and wear jewelry."[28]

When a woman is also a mother or a mother-to-be, she faces additional barriers to advancement and fair treatment in other aspects of her job.

Working mothers

The term "statistical discrimination" refers to the practice of making a decision about an individual because he or she is part of a certain group. In the case of young women, employers have refused to hire women of childbearing age or women with young children "under the assumption that motherhood will cause women to miss more work than men or lead to higher turnover rates."[29] This is now illegal, and in fact employment interviewers are forbidden to even ask a woman if she has or is planning to have children.

Although not mandated by the federal government, many individual companies across the country have established flexible working hours for mothers. A tiny percentage subsidize day-care programs either on-site or nearby. The Pregnancy Discrimination Act (PDA) of 1978 forbids discrimination because of pregnancy. A woman cannot be refused or fired from a job because she is currently pregnant or intends to become pregnant. The law says that pregnancy must be treated the same as any other temporary disability, but an employer may still grant a pregnant woman or new mother a more generous maternity leave package. The Supreme Court said that the PDA provides "a floor beneath which pregnancy disability benefits may not drop—not a ceiling above which they may not rise."[30]

In 1993, as one of his first acts in office, President Bill Clinton signed the Family and Medical Leave Act

(FMLA), which his predecessors had vetoed for many years. Based on the size of the company, the FMLA grants employees the right to take up to a specified number of weeks of leave if they have been with the company for at least a thousand hours over a twelve-month period. During the first part of the leave the employee will be paid a percentage of her salary, and she then has the option of taking a finite period of unpaid time off, with the guarantee that her job will still be waiting for her. This leave can be taken in the event of a birth, adoption, or illness in the family.

Most women find that balancing a career and a family is not easy, and many feel that their rights are being curtailed.

A woman protests the fate of a postal worker who was denied a job because she was pregnant. Many women believe that motherhood and pregnancy in no way impede their ability to hold physically demanding jobs.

A common complaint is that on her return from an extended maternity leave a woman is treated differently by her employer, who may believe the employee no longer values the job highly or can no longer put as much effort into it. Employers may choose to redirect important assignments to other coworkers or take specific responsibilities away from the employee who has been on leave. These acts serve to keep the new mother from being promoted as quickly as she would otherwise have been. Women argue that they are being discriminated against because new fathers do not face the same treatment at their jobs. According to one woman who worked until the day her child was born and then returned to the office three months later, "You either make the decision to stick it out on the fast track or you drop out and you don't get back on. There's a big talent pool out there, and you're easily replaced."[31] She firmly believes that she would not have been promoted if she took even a little more time off. Sociologists point out that because mothers are almost always the primary caregivers, they will, to some degree, have to sacrifice either aspects of their home life or of their work life to accommodate both. That does not mean, however, that employers can decide for the working mother just what she can or cannot handle.

Sexual harassment

In response to high-profile cases like Anita Hill's allegations of sexual harassment against Judge Clarence Thomas at his Supreme Court confirmation hearing and Paula Jones's claim against President Clinton, sexual harassment has become a major issue in America. A New York Times/CBS News poll revealed that four out of ten women said they had been victims of some type of sexual harassment at work, and five out of ten men admitted they had said or done something that could be construed as harassment. But only one out of ten of the women who were harassed felt they would get justice if they reported it. Between 1990 and 1996, the number of sexual harassment claims filed with the Equal Employment Opportunity Commission more than doubled. In 1996 alone, 15,300 workers across the country claimed harassment, but only a small fraction of cases reached a courtroom.

Initially, sexual harassment was considered by the courts to be a personal issue between two individuals, not to be settled in court. Then, in 1976, a case called *Williams v. Saxbe* changed such cases' status. When a woman was fired after refusing her boss's sexual advances, the court agreed that she had been a victim of sexual discrimination and her rights were therefore protected under Title VII of the 1964 Civil Rights Act. In 1977 the courts decided that a woman could now sue the corporate entity that employed her (not just the individual or individuals who harassed her) as long as she could prove that the harassment jeopardized her job. In 1980 the EEOC established a set of guidelines that expanded the definition of sexual harassment. The guidelines state that harassment on the basis of sex is a violation of the law. Unwelcome sexual advances, requests for sexual favors, and other verbal or physical conduct of a sexual nature constitute sexual harassment when submission is implied to be a term or condition of a woman's job; if a woman's job is at stake if she does not comply; or if an intimidating, hostile, or offensive working environment is created. In recent cases this has included the display of pornography and the use of suggestive or lewd language. A woman no longer has to prove that the harassment caused her financial or lasting psychological harm, only that the situation was abusive and caused emotional stress.

Costly lawsuits

According to Donna Harper, a senior trial attorney for the EEOC, "the courts now recognize that employers have a duty to protect employees from unwelcome sexual conduct"[32] and it is clearly in an employer's best interest financially to ensure that sexual harassment does not occur. A 1988 report showed that the nation's top companies lose as much as $6.7 million annually from absenteeism, turnover, and lost productivity due to sexual harassment. Furthermore, in a 1994 landmark sexual harassment case, a jury awarded an employee of a Missouri Wal-Mart store $50 million and found her manager guilty of using abusive language toward her, continuously harassing and intimidating her. The judge later reduced the award to $5 million, but a precedent had been set. The employee told the jury that Wal-Mart had an excellent policy against sexual harassment, but it "just refused to enforce it."[33] In a California case, a jury awarded a secretary at a law firm $7.7 million in damages (later reduced to $3.5 million), or 10 percent of her firm's total worth, finding her employer negligent in protecting its employee from harassment.

Many women are hesitant to come forward with harassment charges because trial testimony can be quite personal. A woman may find her private life, clothing style, and sexual history being used against her in court. In the most talked-about corporate sexual harassment case in recent history, in which hundreds of female employees are suing Mitsubishi Motor Manufacturing of America, a company lawyer sought but was denied the psychological and gynecological records of twenty-nine of the women to distribute to the company's executives. Lynn Hecht Schafran, director of the National Judicial Education Program, speculates on the defendant's tactics: "They'll say 'she's a nut, she made the whole thing up.' Or, 'she's a slut—she asked for it, she enjoyed it.' The idea is to inflict pain on the plaintiff to persuade her to withdraw or settle [the case] for very little [money]."[34]

As a new generation of men and women enter the workforce in even numbers, sociologists are confident that the outcome will be greater equality between the sexes. When discrimination or harassment does occur, women now have unprecedented legal safeguards to protect them.

4

Violence Against Women

VIOLENCE AGAINST WOMEN—in the forms of rape, sexual assault, domestic violence, and murder—is a huge problem in America today. At least every six minutes a woman is raped. One in four female college students will be a victim of rape or sexual assault. Every year 6.2 million women are victims of domestic violence (the actual or threatened physical, sexual, psychological, or economic abuse of an individual by someone with whom they currently have or have had an intimate relationship), and half of the women killed each year are killed by their husband or boyfriend. The Department of Justice estimates that 95 percent of domestic assaults are committed by men against women, and the federal government recently acknowledged that special attention to this issue is desperately needed. In 1994, Congress passed the Violence Against Women Act (VAWA) as part of the largest crime bill in history, the federal Violent Crime Control and Law Enforcement Act. VAWA attempts to combat violence against women in all its facets. First, it provides an unprecedented $1.6 billion over a period of six years to aid police, prosecutors, prevention programs, and victims of sexual violence or domestic abuse. Second, new laws carry stricter punishments for offenders and greatly increase the chances that the crime will be prosecuted to the full extent of the law. Third, new rights have been granted to the victim to protect her from further harm, both physical and psycho-

Members of the National Organization for Women hold a rally in support of laws that protect women against violence.

logical, and to ease the painful process of reporting and prosecuting the crime, both emotionally and financially. A final part of the bill, the Jacob Wetterling Act, protects women and children from released rapists and other violent offenders by requiring that local law enforcement authorities keep current data on their whereabouts.

The sponsor of the bill, Senator Joseph Biden, calls it

> the first comprehensive approach to fighting all forms of violence against women, combining a broad array of needed reforms. . . . I have become convinced that violence against women reflects as much a failure of our nation's collective moral imagination as it does the failure of our nation's laws and regulations.[35]

In March 1995, President Clinton named Bonnie Campbell, former attorney general of Iowa, to be director of the Violence Against Women Office at the Department of Justice. The office is charged with ensuring that the Violence Against Women Act is upheld and that information and funds are properly funneled to the states and local organizations. Since most sexual offenses are prosecuted in state courts, it is up to the states to enact laws consistent with the federal VAWA and to apply for the grants the federal government is offering. It is a slow process, but many states are already strengthening their laws and their law enforcement policies in accordance with the new federal regulations.

Strengthening law enforcement's role

The largest amount of money will be funneled into law enforcement training. From 1994 to the year 2000, $800 million will go toward training police, prosecutors, and judges in their responsibilities pertaining to violence against women. Many people faced with acts of violence against women feel that the criminal justice system is biased in favor of the offender. Police are accused of being unwilling to get involved in domestic disputes, lawyers are accused of convincing victims to drop rape charges because they are hard to prove, and judges are accused of being too lenient on offenders. According to Senator Biden, obstacles to a fair trial exist on many levels: "The problem is rooted not only in inadequacies in the law, but in the pervasive prejudices against victims of [violence against women] by everyone from members of the jury to police to prosecutors to judges."[36] Recent state gender-bias studies by the Maryland Special Joint Committee on Gender Bias in the Courts found that "too often judges and court employees deny the victim's experiences, accuse the victim of lying about her injuries, and treat the cases as trivial and unimportant."[37]

To combat this problem, VAWA has allocated funds to law enforcement groups in all fifty states to assist them in restructuring their response to crimes of violence against women. The program is called STOP, and it requires state law enforcement personnel, prosecutors, and victim service providers to collaborate in an effort to better understand these crimes and how they should be dealt with in court. The funds will help train law enforcement officers, increase the number of personnel in law enforcement and district attorneys' offices that target violence against women, develop more effective policies to prevent such violence, and apply advanced technology to improve communications systems that will identify and track arrests and prosecutions as well as keep track of victim protection mechanisms like restraining orders. Another program called Community Policing to Combat Domestic Violence provides for one hundred thousand more law enforcement officials on the streets of America specifically to work towards handling domestic violence.

Improving shelters and rape crisis centers

Domestic violence is the single most common cause of injury to women, greater than car accidents, stranger rapes, and mugging combined. Statistics show that a woman is nine times more likely to become a victim of violence in her own home than on the street. The main reason women stay in violent situations, experts report, is because they believe they have nowhere else to go. VAWA allocates $325 million toward improving the services offered by battered women's shelters, an important part of helping a

A woman at a demonstration against domestic violence holds a sign in memory of her granddaughter, who was killed by her boyfriend.

woman escape from recurrent violence at home. The funds are important because, according to a Ford Foundation report, 50 percent of all homeless women and children in the United States are running away from domestic violence. Shelters help keep victims off the streets by providing a safe place where a woman's batterer cannot reach her. Trained counselors assist the women in handling their situation and alert them of their legal options. The government funding will allow more shelters to open and will strengthen existing shelters in need of more staff, more supplies, and more beds.

Prevention and education to reduce sexual assaults

A 1990 Senate committee report indicated that at some point during their lives, three out of four women will be victims of a violent crime. Educators stress that women need to know how to protect themselves from becoming

DOMESTIC VIOLENCE

victims and also what steps to take after an assault. Approximately $205 million is going toward programs directed at the education and prevention of violence against women, including educational seminars, professional training programs, expanding community programs, and preparing and distributing informational materials. Educating youth is an important part of this appropriation, with $400,000 targeted for violence against women education within the schools. Thirty million dollars will go toward educating, treating, and counseling youth who are at particularly high risk of sexual abuse. This includes runaways, children living on the streets, prostitutes, and children who have been past victims of abuse.

National hotlines

Over the past decade, many local hotlines have been set up around the country for women to call to report abuse or get on-the-spot counseling. In the wake of the murder of Nicole Brown Simpson, calls to domestic violence hotlines have increased across the nation by as much as 80 percent. These small operations, usually run by volunteers, have little money for overhead and often operate within a very small calling area. In 1995 President Clinton initiated the National Domestic Violence Hotline to function as a centralized resource for women in crisis. This project has been allocated $3 million to provide callers with crisis intervention. Counselors can refer callers to emergency services and shelters in their area or connect them with their local police department. This hotline is joined by the Rape Abuse Incest National Network (RAINN), a private-sector toll-free hotline that connects the caller to local crisis centers. Congress declared May 16, 1997, National RAINN Day in support of private organizations' efforts to make a difference in helping victims of sexual violence.

Legal ramifications of violence against women

Traditionally, rape and domestic violence cases have been hard to prosecute because they often disintegrate into

one person's word against the other. One report found that "police are reluctant to arrest batterers, prosecutors are hesitant to try them in court, and judges are unlikely to impose harsh settlements on them."[38] According to a 1992 report from the Senate Judiciary Committee, the rate of rape in the 1980s rose four times faster than the total crime rate. Rape counselors estimate that over 1.2 million women are raped each year, but official estimates are around 500,000. Only 16 percent of these women report the crime to the police and only half the cases are brought to court. In the absence of strict and specific laws, sentencing for rape and other sexually violent crimes has historically been light. According to a study by Brandeis University, at least 90 percent of batterers are never prosecuted. Twenty-five percent of convicted rapists are never incarcerated, while another 25 percent only serve an average of eleven months in local jails. Lynn Hecht Schafran, director of the National Judicial Education Program at the National Organization for Women, explains that "because sex offenders often have no other criminal record, judges may consider the rape an aberration and the defendant deserving of lenient treatment."[39]

Tougher sentences

Under VAWA "repeat offender" section, if an offender is convicted of a sexual crime after one or more prior convictions, his maximum term of imprisonment will double. Furthermore, there is now a "three strikes" category, which mandates life imprisonment without possibility of parole for an offender's third conviction for a violent felony (or drug trafficking crime). Rape is now considered a violent felony along with such offenses as murder and kidnapping. Since the O. J. Simpson case, every state has passed or proposed some type of new domestic violence legislation. In California, no longer can a first-time offender have his record cleared if he attends a counseling program. In Rhode Island, a second-time offender must serve at least ten days in prison. After that, subsequent offenses result in a minimum of one year in jail.

Furthermore, when domestic violence crosses state boundaries it is now punishable as a federal offense. Previously, each state where the violence occurred was very limited in what it could do because of jurisdictional problems. The first case prosecuted under VAWA is an example of what qualifies as interstate domestic violence under this new ruling. In November 1994 a West Virginia man named Christopher Bailey beat his wife, Sonya, until she collapsed. He then put her in the trunk of their car and drove for five days across West Virginia and Kentucky, stopping along the way to withdraw money from their accounts and to purchase adult diapers for Sonya. She was eventually brought to an emergency room in Kentucky, and remains in a permanent vegetative state with irreversible brain damage. Bailey was arrested in Kentucky, but the police dropped the charges since they could not document what had actually occurred in that state. If Bailey were simply prosecuted back in West Virginia, he may have received less than a two-year sentence. But under the new federal law, he was sentenced to life in prison for the abuse and kidnapping of his wife.

Protection to victims of gender-based violence

In the past few years the law has come a long way toward protecting the victim from her attacker and relieving her from additional financial and emotional burdens and from further abuse when she enters a courtroom. Most states now have a policy that police must arrest a domestic assault offender if a family member was assaulted and probable cause for arrest exists. The same mandatory arrest follows if there is probable cause that a protection order has been violated. Rita Smith, director of the National Coalition Against Domestic Violence, says that her organization pushed for these laws so police have no option but to arrest when they see evidence of abuse. These provisions relieve the police of having to determine exactly what happened before securing the victim from further immediate harm.

Since the 1960s, mandatory reporting practices have been in place to force doctors, nurses, and teachers to report suspicions of physical and sexual abuse to the police. But a study in the early 1990s found that 53 percent of the 143 accredited medical schools in the United States and Canada did not require medical students to be instructed on how to handle the discovery of domestic violence. One report showed that in 40 percent of the domestic violence cases presented in emergency rooms the treating physician did not even discuss the abuse with the patient, though the cause of the injuries was known. Many hospitals have set up protocols to follow in domestic violence cases since they realize that merely treating a victim's injuries and sending the patient home makes the health care system part of the problem, not part of the solution. But compliance has proven difficult: A study in a major metropolitan hospital with domestic violence protocols in place found that only in 8 percent of abuse cases did anyone talk to the woman about her situation or address concerns for her safety.

Another measure intended to protect the victim from further harm prohibits a domestic violence offender, or anyone subject to a protection order for harassing, stalking, or threatening an intimate partner or former intimate partner, from purchasing or possessing a firearm or ammunition.

This is an attempt to give the victim a bit more peace of mind. Furthermore, the Full Faith and Credit provision of VAWA says that a protection order issued in one state must also be honored in another state. This means that if at any time the woman has to leave the state, to take shelter with relatives or on business or vacation, she is still officially protected from further contact.

Women at a New York rally express their outrage at violence against women.

A victim's rights in court

The Department of Justice is currently disseminating model legislation to the states making communications between a victim and her support counselor immune from subpoena for use in court. This confidentiality, it is hoped, would give an abused woman more confidence to turn to rape crisis centers or battered women's shelters and to report the crime. At trial, however, in most states judges still have the right to use what is called "Lord Hale" instructions—the judge instructs the jury prior to beginning the case that the charge of rape is easily made and hard to prove. The judge then urges the jury to carefully examine the victim's testimony before returning a verdict. Studies have shown that this speech can prejudice the jury against the victim, and the federal government is urging state courts to ban this discriminatory practice. One major step toward not "putting the victim on trial" has been the use of so-called Rape Shields, now in place nationwide, to seal the victim's sexual past, psychological history, and medical records from court exposure. Also, before VAWA, lawyers were not allowed to present the jury with the accused rapist's previous rape convictions. Women believed that the courts were protecting the rapist instead of the woman's right to use all available, clearly relevant information in her defense. Now those records are admissible

Students at Bard College in New York protest the college's policy regarding sexual assault and harassment. College campuses have a high incidence of rape and sexual assault.

evidence to show the man's patterns of behavior and to establish his identity. This gives more credence to the woman's story and offsets the "it's his word against hers" factor, which can keep the jury from returning a conviction. Battered wives can now point to evidence of past abuse to support claims of a pattern of violence. Furthermore, a victim of a federal violent or sexual abuse crime now has the right to address the court prior to the sentencing of her assailant. If the victim is under eighteen years old, a parent or legal guardian can speak for her. If she is deceased or incapacitated, this right is extended to other family members.

Date rape, sexual assault, and rape by a stranger occurs at a higher rate on college campuses than anywhere else, but less than 20 percent of campus rapes are prosecuted in the criminal court system. A study in 1991 revealed that universities only punish 36 percent of the perpetrators and that punishment is often no stronger than suspension for a semester and could be as lenient as a warning. In an effort to address these inequities, the 1992 federal Student Right to Know and Campus Security Act makes colleges accountable for the number of rapes on campus and for the security measures they are taking to prevent sexual violence. Campus administrators could no longer downplay or hide these figures to protect the school's reputation at the expense of female students' safety. Many schools have now created legislation modeled on Antioch College's Sexual Consent Policy of 1992, in which the rules of consensual sexual encounters are clearly spelled out. If they are violated, the women have grounds to accuse the men of sexual assault and specific punishments are set up accordingly. One young woman, Katie Koestner, tours the country's universities speaking out on the injustice of downplaying the severity of date rape. "I am a survivor of rape," she tells groups of young people. "And I will not be silent. I tell my story every day because deans at colleges around this country have told me that date rape is 'an unfortunate miscommunication.'"[40] Sexual violence on campuses is being monitored more closely by the government now, which helps ensure that date rape on campus will be prosecuted as strongly as rape by a stranger.

Relieving the victim's financial burden

Every state had to agree that within two years of the signing of VAWA, the victims of sexual assault will not have to pay to file criminal charges or for protection orders. The states must also agree to pay all costs for forensic medical examinations for victims of rape and sexual violence just as they would for all other criminal investigations.

If a victim decides to prosecute her attacker, it can cost her thousands of dollars. Now, once the attacker is charged with the crime, he is responsible for paying the full amount of the victim's losses for the crime committed against her. This includes court and attorney fees, medical bills relating to physical and psychiatric care, even income that the victim lost during the ordeal. For the first time, a victim of a gender-motivated crime may also sue her attacker for damages on top of these costs.

Protecting society at large

VAWA introduced the Jacob Wetterling Guidelines, which provide the states with a financial incentive to keep

Women participate in a Take Back the Night demonstration to protest sexual harassment, date rape, and other forms of mistreatment toward women.

records of the locations of convicted rapists, sexual offenders, and child molesters. Upon release from prison, sexual offenders must register with local state law enforcement agencies for the next ten years or until the state deems they are no longer a threat. Failure to register is a criminal offense. These protocols will help state agencies keep track of sex offenders who cross state lines, and may inhibit offenders from committing more crimes since the police know exactly who and where they are. The agencies are also expected to alert the community to the location of the offender when deemed necessary for public safety.

Once a year the National Organization for Women sponsors a nationwide march called Take Back the Night. This rally, held in cities and on college campuses all across the country, is an effort to raise public awareness of the increasing prevalence of violence against women, and to empower women to do what they can to prevent being victimized. During this one night, women can walk the streets without fear. The hope is that one day women really will be able to take back the night, every night.

5

Reproductive Rights

WOMEN'S UNIQUE ABILITY to bear children gives rise to a number of controversial issues concerning their right to decide when and if to give birth. Opinion ranges from making sure all women have access to birth control to prevent pregnancy, and access to abortion if they choose to terminate their pregnancy, to placing limits on women's reproductive choices, especially on abortion. Currently a woman's reproductive rights are subject to federal and state legislation and Supreme Court decisions.

The beginning of birth control

In the 1990s, women take it for granted that birth control is widely available at any drugstore. But it took the relentless perseverance of one woman, Margaret Sanger, and a group of ardent supporters to convince the government that women should have the right to control their reproduction. One of eleven children, Margaret Sanger was a nurse in the early 1900s when she witnessed the financial, physical, and emotional burden large families imposed on mothers and society. One incident incited her to help women limit childbearing. A young mother who was very ill due to complications of her pregnancy came to Sanger's office. The doctor told her not to get pregnant again, but when she begged him to tell her how, he just shrugged and jokingly told her to tell her husband to sleep on the roof. Even though medical doctors knew about birth control, they had no power to distribute it. Soon the woman was back in the office, pregnant again and very ill. This time she died.

Sanger vowed to get the word out about contraception because "no woman can call herself free until she can choose consciously whether she will or will not be a mother."[41]

Believing that women were oppressed by their inability to control their own reproduction, Sanger set out on a crusade to give them this right. With the help of friends she coined the phrase "birth control" to mean any action taken to prevent pregnancy. Supporters of hers formed the National Birth Control League in 1915, and she herself founded the American Birth Control League in 1921. Later these would combine to form the Planned Parenthood Federation, which now has clinics all over the world to educate women and to provide them with birth control and medical services. Sanger gave speeches across the nation, published information on the reproductive process and contraception, and opened America's first birth control clinic in 1916. Her pamphlets were considered quite graphic; explaining the functions of a woman's body in such an open way was considered lewd at that time. She was jailed nine times for violating the Comstock laws, which were in place to suppress material considered to be obscene or indecent. Each time she was arrested she came out stronger and more determined.

Hard-earned victory

In 1937, the U.S. attorney general said that birth control could be legally imported into America, and the American Medical Association decided to support birth control and public sex education. Before turning her sights on the international birth control movement, Sanger made sure even the smallest farming village in America had access to birth control by setting up local outposts where women could go to be educated and receive contraceptives. As Sanger prepared to focus on the need for birth control around the world, she was praised by Professor Norman Himes of Colgate University, the author of a major population study. Himes declared that "No reformer in human history—and I weigh my words well—no reformer has lived to see the things she stood for so completely brought about."[42]

In 1965 the Supreme Court ruled in *Griswold v. Connecticut*, a case questioning Connecticut's right to restrict access to birth control, that the Constitution provides citizens with a "zone of privacy" that protects certain practices from governmental intrusion. It found, therefore, that Connecticut had violated the rights of married people by not making contraception available. Later, the Court extended the same right of privacy to minors and other unmarried people, guaranteeing them access to contraception as well. After this, any state that had a law against contraception was forced to rescind it.

The Food and Drug Administration (FDA) was given the responsibility of approving the research and marketing of new birth control drugs or devices. The birth control pill gained approval in the 1960s, and by the end of the decade one out of every three women used it. The invention of "the Pill" was considered a landmark event for women because it offered a simple and reliable way for them to be in full control of their reproduction.

Margaret Sanger waits to speak before a Senate subcommittee regarding a bill to legalize a physician's right to discuss birth control with patients.

Emergency contraception

The role of the FDA is to protect the public from potentially dangerous products by carefully testing and evaluating a new drug or device for safety before allowing distribution in the United States. This means that even though a woman has the right to use whatever birth control method she chooses, the FDA must first approve it. Certain forms of birth control approved for use in other countries are not available in the United States, including a pill called RU486. Approved in Europe, RU486 has been used for nearly a decade. It is commonly referred to as the "morning-after" pill, because it allows a woman to prevent implantation in the uterus of a potentially fertilized egg if she thinks her birth control method failed. It will also work up to seven weeks by expelling the embryo from the uterus.

RU486 has not gained FDA approval for sale or use in America due to safety concerns as well as pressure from antiabortion groups. The FDA believes that not enough evidence is available to verify its safety, and antiabortionists claim that it is functionally a form of abortion, and that women will take advantage of the ease of this method if it becomes available. The FDA is still debating the risks involved with the drug, but in the meantime has released research showing that many brands of regular birth control pills, if taken in high dosages within three days after unprotected sex, could effectively stop the potentially fertilized egg from implanting in the womb. Against the wishes of antiabortionists, the FDA gave approval for the Pill to be used for this purpose and is urging doctors and pharmaceutical companies to let women know this option exists. According to FDA commissioner David Kessler, "The best-kept contraceptive secret is no longer a secret. Women should have the information that this regimen is available."[43] Research by James Trussell at Princeton University convinced the FDA that using the Pill this way could prevent up to 2.3 million unplanned pregnancies annually, a million of which would otherwise end in abortion.

Members of NOW and the Christian Coalition express opposing views on the importation of the birth control drug RU486. The drug is controversial because it aborts a potentially fertilized egg.

Abortion rights

The intentional removal of a fetus from the womb before it is able to survive on its own is called abortion. In America, abortion rights is a controversial issue. In 1973, the Supreme Court legalized abortion throughout America by ruling that women have a constitutional right to decide whether to terminate a pregnancy. This decision, handed down in *Roe v. Wade*, also acknowledged the role of the individual states to regulate abortion. It states that during the first trimester of pregnancy (the first twelve weeks) the states could not forbid abortions. During the second trimester (thirteen to twenty-four weeks) the states could only restrict abortion if the mother's health was endangered. But after twenty-four weeks came the stage of "fetal viability," at which point it is possible that a fetus can survive outside the womb. At this stage, unless the procedure was necessary to save the woman's life or protect her from serious health problems, the states had the right to restrict or ban abortion in order to protect the unborn child.

The government effectively saved women from a potentially dangerous situation by legalizing abortion. Before this ruling, abortions were performed illegally, often by untrained abortionists using crude tools. This led to many reports of serious injury and even death. The procedure is now performed by qualified doctors in carefully monitored facilities. In the years since the decision was handed down, the government continues to restrict women's rights to abortion by amending the Supreme Court's ruling.

Narrowing *Roe v. Wade*

In 1976, Congress passed the Hyde Amendment, which after some revision now says that federal Medicaid funds (money from the government to pay for health care for the poor) can only be used for abortion services if the woman's life is at stake, or, in some states, if the pregnancy is the result of rape or incest. The Supreme Court stood behind the Hyde Amendment, saying that just because a woman has a right to have an abortion does not mean she has a right to public funds to pay for it. It added that states can even withhold Medicaid funds for abortions completely, if they choose to do so.

Justice William Brennan, who disagreed with the Hyde Amendment, believed it violated *Roe v. Wade*'s ruling that the federal government must "refrain from wielding its enormous power and influence in a manner that might burden the pregnant woman's freedom to choose whether to

Women in support of abortion convene outside the Supreme Court building in commemoration of the twenty-second anniversary of Roe v. Wade.

have an abortion."[44] Justice Thurgood Marshall, also dissenting, said that "it is a cruel blow to the most powerless members of our society," and that he feared the restriction would force poor women "to resort to back-alley butchers, attempt to induce an abortion themselves by crude and dangerous methods, or suffer the serious medical consequences of attempting to carry the fetus to term."[45] Some states, in order to avoid making these fears a reality, are choosing to continue to fund abortions for women unable to pay for them themselves, regardless of the federal restrictions.

Reproductive Health Services of Missouri, Planned Parenthood, and three individual health care workers challenged the constitutionality of the state of Missouri's legislation in 1986 concerning fetuses and abortions. In 1989 the case, entitled *Webster v. Reproductive Health Services*, reached the Supreme Court, which ruled in favor of the state. The decision stopped short of overturning *Roe v. Wade*, but did give individual states the right to impose their own restrictions on abortion as they saw fit to protect potential life. They could forbid public hospitals or federally funded clinics from performing abortions (unless to save the woman's life) or even from discussing the option of abortion with their patients. Doctors were now told they had to determine—through testing or otherwise—if the fetus was viable (able to live on its own) as early as twenty weeks into the pregnancy, which was during the second trimester. Many states tried to push the limits of restriction until they were challenged in court and forced to put a cap on their control.

The consequences

In all, over five hundred new abortion restrictions were created by state legislatures in the wake of the *Webster* ruling. Planned Parenthood of Southeastern Pennsylvania brought suit against Pennsylvania's new Abortion Control Act, claiming it was unconstitutional. The case reached the Supreme Court in 1992 and the Court, as in *Webster*, decided in favor of the state. This strengthened the government's previous decision to allow the states to set their own rules. States now have the right to impose a twenty-four-to-forty-eight-hour delay on abortion and to insist the woman receives state-mandated information discouraging abortion. In many areas where certain hospitals or clinics perform abortions once a week, critics argue that this mandatory delay could push the woman to a point in her pregnancy when the abortion would no longer be safe or legal.

Women and men march in Washington, D.C., to protest the anniversary of Roe v. Wade. *The case, which made abortion legal in all fifty states, remains highly controversial.*

A state may now require a young woman under age eighteen to obtain parental consent from one or more parents before having an abortion. In states where a parental involvement law is in place, the Supreme Court said that a "judicial bypass option" must also be in place so a young woman can appeal to a judge in lieu of obtaining permission from a parent. She can then try to convince the judge that either she is mature enough to make the decision on her own, or that it would not be in her best interest to involve her parents. The issue of parental consent is quite controversial. On one hand, no child can undergo any other operation without parental consent, so some parents argue that abortion should not be any different. On the other hand, teenagers argue that it is their life, their body, and it should be their decision. In a publicized Indiana case, seventeen-year-old Becky Bell, saying she loved her parents so much she could not bear to disappoint them by telling them she was pregnant, appealed to a judge who denied her the right to an abortion without parental consent. Desperate, she sought out an unregistered abortionist and underwent the procedure anyway. Complications from the operation led to her death. Her devastated parents have embarked on a nationwide campaign to repeal parental consent laws.

The final obstacle

Since many hospitals can or will no longer perform abortions due to strict state laws, the great majority are performed at clinics. Women entering clinics known to perform abortions are often faced with antiabortion protestors who feel it is their duty to make her reconsider her decision. The protesters might carry signs or hand out flyers indicating that they feel abortion is wrong, while pleading with the woman to change her mind based on their own religious or moral belief that abortion is a form of murder. Some protesters are very aggressive. They may block the doorway of the clinic so the woman must push through them or leave. Many incidents have been reported where "altercations and aggressive counseling often developed into 'in your face' yelling, and sometimes into pushing, shoving and grabbing."[46]

Armed with slogans and an empty crib, a group of antiabortionists gather in front of a Planned Parenthood office in New York. In 1997, the Supreme Court ruled that demonstrators had to stay at least fifteen feet away from the entrance of abortion clinics to allow women free access.

In an effort to protect women from harassment or violence outside clinics, President Clinton signed the Freedom of Access to Clinics Act in 1994. With this law, anyone protesting outside a clinic, no matter how unobtrusive he or she is, is subject to arrest. This idea, while protecting clinic clients from psychological trauma and potential harm, violates the First Amendment, which gives everyone the freedom to speak their minds. Because of this dilemma, the act is not often enforced. In 1997, the Supreme Court tried to define the law better by forbidding demonstrators to be within a fifteen-foot "fixed buffer zone" of the doorways or driveways of abortion clinics. The Court did, however, allow two protesters at a time to enter the buffer zone to persuade a woman not to go through with her scheduled appointment as long as it is in a nonthreatening way. But if the woman requests that the "sidewalk counselors," as they are known, leave her alone, they must "cease and desist" and return back outside the buffer zone. Vicki Saporta, executive director of the National Abortion Federation, a trade association of abortion providers, is very pleased with the Court's decision and said, "We see the fixed buffer zone as the key element in protecting clinics."[47]

Serious threats to doctors and staff

Not only the safety of the women receiving abortions, but also the safety of abortion providers and medical staff is often in jeopardy. By 1995 three doctors along with two receptionists and an aide, had been murdered by zealous opponents of abortion. The National Abortion Federation, in an effort to warn women of the serious threats to their freedom, reports that between 1993 and 1994 there were 8 attempted murders, 4 bombings, 14 cases of arson, 11 attempts at bombing and arson, 153 counts of vandalism,

Abortion clinic volunteers shield a patient under an umbrella to protect her from being harassed by antiabortion protesters.

128 death threats, and 204 cases of stalking, all in the name of protecting the unborn child. Besides creating an atmosphere of fear and hostility, these actions further hamper a woman's access to abortion and the legal right of the doctor to perform it. In 1992 the *New York Times* reported that the only doctor left in South Dakota who performs abortions "works in a cinderblock office with bullet-proof windows and burglar alarms. For eleven years he has had to walk through pickets to enter his office."[48]

In 1995, antistalking and trespassing laws enacted in many states now protect citizens from unwanted contact. An Oregon antistalking law set a precedent throughout the country: In 1996, the leader of a large national antiabortion group called Advocates for Life Ministries was found guilty of stalking and threatening the executive director of the All Women's Health Services clinic and was ordered to permanently stay away from her. His permit to carry concealed weapons was also revoked.

Few issues are as volatile as the right to abortion. As long as public opinion is divided, a woman's right to elect to have an abortion may continue to be challenged.

6

The Plight of Women Around the Globe

YOUNG PEOPLE IN the United States today are growing up in a society where equality is the goal and discrimination, if brought to light, does not go unpunished. The historical notion of women's inferiority to men is becoming part of our nation's past, not its present or future. In many other countries around the world, however, women still lack even the most basic rights. Some women do not have the right to vote, to go to school, or to hold a job. Many are not protected from discrimination, sexual harassment, or gender-based violence.

In September 1995, 189 countries sent representatives to Beijing, China, to attend the United Nations' Fourth World Conference on Women. Their job was to create a plan for the international community to advance the status of women. The result was the Platform for Action, focusing on three major areas: fostering economic advancement, securing equal rights and access to education and health care, and ending violence against women and girls. Since creating new programs is expensive, the delegates agreed to aid developing countries in achieving these goals. James D. Wolfensohn, the president of the World Bank, announced that World Bank has already set aside $200 million in loans to help women escape poverty and start their own businesses. It will also slate about $5 billion of the $20 billion it lends each year to specifically address the concerns of women.

Recognizing that each country has its own cultural practices and traditions, Hillary Rodham Clinton urged the attendees to band together for the common good in her convention speech:

> However different we may be, there is far more that unites us than divides us. We share a common future, and we are here to find common ground so that we may help bring new dignity and respect to women and girls all over the world—and in so doing, bring new strength and stability to families as well.[48]

As a reporter for the *Philadelphia Inquirer* pointed out, "Often what is justified as cultural tradition is only a reflection of local belief that the female is worth less than the male."[49] By the year 2000, each country is supposed to show a marked improvement in the way its society treats women. As of now, there is a long way to go.

Women and education

Without the right or opportunity to be educated, women are effectively kept on the outskirts of a functioning society. There are 960 million people around the world who are illiterate—unable to read or write. Two-thirds of them are women. Girls make up two-thirds of the children in the world without access to even a primary education. It is very common in the less industrialized countries for girls to be taken out of school early so they can help with the domestic chores while their brothers continue to be educated. Early marriage and teenage pregnancy also account for young girls leaving school early.

Female delegates attend the United Nations' Fourth World Conference on Women in 1995.

In many large industrialized nations like the United States, girls have as many educational opportunities as boys. The difference may be found in the paths their educations take. In Japan, for instance, a primary concern of Japanese parents is to find their daughter a husband. With that in mind, girls are encouraged to go to college to meet potential mates, but also to study subjects in the arts and literature to broaden their minds. They are still expected to be a wife and mother upon graduation.

Afghanistan, now ruled by a Muslim militia group called the Taliban, has the world's most restrictive policy regarding education for women. Basically, girls are no longer allowed to attend school at all, and no girl over ten years old can leave the house without being accompanied by a male relative. At the former Malili High School for Girls in the capital city of Kabul, the girls used to study amid broken windows and desks cracked as the result of so many years of Afghanistan's civil war. When the Taliban took over, the girls were all sent home, and the school was closed. The government plans to reopen it as a *madrasah*—a religious school for boys. In support of keeping girls at home with their mothers, the new education minister recently explained that a woman is "like a rose—you water it and keep it at home for yourself to look at and smell. It is not supposed to be taken out of the house to be smelled."[50]

Women, the workplace, and economic freedom

Women and girls make up 70 percent of the billion people in the world who live in poverty. In much of the world, women are either not allowed to work at all, leaving them at the mercy of husbands or male relatives, or are unable to secure anything other than low-paying jobs. Sociologists call this situation "the feminization of poverty." In America, women are still fighting for laws guaranteeing them equal access to jobs and equality in the workplace, but many other countries are far behind. In Japan, where nearly a third of the women reported being sexually harassed but only a handful have ever filed lawsuits, change is slow in coming. Japanese working women earn 57 percent of what their male counterparts earn and constitute only 0.3 percent of the boards of large corporations. To amend the situation, the government passed the Equal Employment Opportunities Bill to end discrimination based

In Japan women office workers are subjected to more sexual harassment than their American counterparts.

on sex in 1985, but companies are not punished for failing to adhere to its policies. Many young, educated Japanese women continue to work as "office flowers" who are "expected to serve their male co-workers with green tea ten times a day, and to devote the rest of their energies to photocopying or looking pretty."[51] They are usually not eligible for promotions and are expected to leave after they marry. In China the situation is not much different in terms of advancement. Most women are kept in low-paying clerical or factory jobs. According to one Chinese woman, when she and her husband married they were both ordinary workers. While she is not able to rise above her factory job, he now manages a private trading firm in a modern office and owns a mobile phone.

In Russia, according to the Moscow Center for Gender Studies, women earned only 40 percent of what men earned in 1995. In some areas, 85 percent of unemployed workers are women and 90 percent of female college graduates cannot find work. According to Martina Vandenberg, who works with nongovernmental organizations in Russia and Ukraine, "The only thing Russian women have of value in the market is sex."[52] The women, trapped between not working at all or sacrificing their pride, are all too often forced to offer sexual services in exchange for a steady office job. A typical job-search ad reads: "Twenty-three-year-old girl, admirable in every way, great measurements, well-built, efficient, communicative . . . seeks serious work as a secretary-abstractor. . . . I will be an ornament in your office."[53] The ads end either with the phrase "*bez intima*" which means "no intimate relationships," or "*bez kompleksov*," which means "without complexes." The latter, which lets the employer know that the woman is willing to become sexually involved, is so common that it is often simply abbreviated as "*b/k*."

Forbidden to work

In many countries, however, the women have even less economic freedom. In Saudi Arabia, women have a hard time commuting to work since they are not allowed to drive. The right to own or inherit property is forbidden in many countries; and in Muslim countries, girls usually inherit only half as much as their brothers. Under the new Taliban government in Afghanistan, women are no longer allowed to work at all. One woman explained to *Time* magazine that the situation is especially hard on all the war

Women's Wages as % of Men's*

Country	%
Costa Rica	74%
Egypt	68
El Salvador	94
Hong Kong	69
Kenya	74
Paraguay	66
South Korea	50
Zambia	73

*manufacturing

widows who now have no way of supporting their families. In another Muslim country, Algeria, the Algerian Islamic Salvation Front is now trying to get a law passed that would also forbid a woman to work outside the home at all.

Women and reproductive rights

It took the efforts of dedicated women like Margaret Sanger to convince the people of America that women should be allowed to participate in family planning. Today women can openly receive information about contraception to figure out what method is best for them, and insurance carriers, clinics, and hospitals all work to insure that women have safe childbirth. In many parts of the world, however, complications related to pregnancy and childbirth are one of the leading causes of mortality among women of reproductive age. Women often do not get the treatment and care they need or hospitals are unequipped to handle emergencies. In six regions of Russia, for example, there were between 85 and 116 maternity-related deaths per 100,000 live births between 1991 and 1992, a rate eight to ten times higher than in European countries.

Different countries have different ways of handling family planning. Abortion is a punishable crime in Catholic

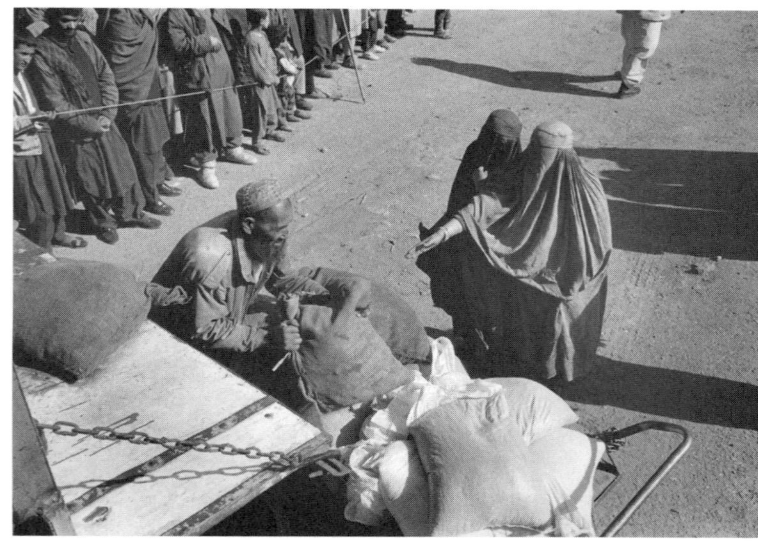

Veiled Afghan women receive food relief. The Taliban, a fundamentalist Muslim sect controlling large areas of Afghanistan, does not allow women to work.

Ireland, but in Russia abortion is the leading form of birth control. In 1992, 206 abortions were performed in Russia for every 100 live births. In China a woman can easily get birth control since, in an effort to reduce the skyrocketing population, each family is only allowed to have one child. Conversely, in Rumania there is a four-child policy that carries with it mandatory gynecological inspections, close monitoring of women's pregnancies, and economic sanctions if women do not comply.

Other countries also restrict women in terms of reproduction. In Japan, condoms can be bought from vending machines on street corners, but the government has banned women from taking control of their own reproduction by restricting use of the birth control pill. In India, Geeta Mukherjee, a member of Parliament who has campaigned for women's rights for decades, says, "Indian society is absolutely male dominated. It is the men who decide how many children [their wives] will have."[54] Human Rights Watch in Washington, D.C., explains that women in India have little control over their lives because they "have second-class status as human beings. Their lives matter so little, people feel they can do whatever they want with them."[55]

Violence in the name of tradition

Worldwide violence against women encompasses physical, sexual, and psychological abuse occurring in the family or within the general community, sometimes perpetrated or condoned by the government.

Terrible acts of violence against women continue to be done in the name of cultural tradition. The practice of female genital mutilation (FGM), performed on girls between the ages of three and thirteen, is still a rite of passage in nearly forty-one countries. Based on a ritual performed in Egypt as much as four thousand years ago, it entails cutting off most or all of a young girl's exterior sexual organs and, in many cases, sewing her vulva almost completely shut to ensure her virginity and diminish her sexual drive. FGM is performed in more than twenty-five

During a women's rights march in New York, a woman protests the custom of genital mutilation. Many African nations still allow the practice.

Muslim nations in Africa, as well as in parts of the Middle East, Southeast Asia, and South America. Affecting more than 100 million women worldwide, six thousand girls are subjected to the surgery—often with little or no anesthetic—every single day. Side effects include terrible pain; shock; recurring infection; hemorrhaging; pelvic diseases; infertility; psychological trauma; painful urination, menstruation, intercourse, and childbirth; and even death. In Somalia, where 99 percent of girls have undergone FGM, one woman explains that "the procedure is proof of your virginity, and men only want to marry virgins."[56] Due to outside pressure, many countries, including Nigeria and Egypt, have recently banned FGM, but so far there is little change. In 1997, a U.S. law refused most loans to countries who continue to perform FGM unless those countries have set up educational programs to end the practice.

In many countries the institution of marriage often brings violence with it. In India a bride's father is expected to come up with a suitable dowry (money or goods) that he will give to his daughter's husband upon her marriage. But when the husbands are not satisfied with the dowry, some wives pay with their lives by having kerosene poured on them and ignited. The Indian government reports that between 1990 and 1996, over twenty thousand brides have been killed over dowry disputes, and researchers believe this is a very low estimate. In fact, in greater Bombay, 25 percent of the girls who die between the age of fifteen and twenty-four are killed in this manner. According to Human Rights Watch, "In the case of dowry deaths, women enter the marriage on unequal footing. They are seen as 'chattel,' as property. So when the woman doesn't bring in the necessary economic reward, the family thinks it is in their right to get rid of her."[57]

In terms of domestic violence, in Iran a man can legally hit his wife, and in Syria the fact that most domestic disagreements are settled with violence is reflected on one of Syria's most popular television shows, where husbands are often shown beating their wives. In India, eight out of ten wives are reportedly victims of domestic battery or dowry-related abuse.

Female infanticide

The killing of female babies is still widespread in both China and India. Female babies are often left to die of starvation or are killed outright. Since in China each couple can only have one child, many prefer boys. Not only is a boy child more valuable as a worker, but many followers of Confucianism believe a man needs a son to help him get to heaven. The World Bank reports that in India, where the population increases by as much as fifty thousand babies a day, every sixth infant death is due to female infanticide. In one area of southern India, infanticide takes place in one out of every two families. The reasons are similar to China's—a girl won't bring in money and the father will have to pay a dowry when she marries. The population in India is so high that after a woman has had three or more children her husband will send her to a sterilization camp where a doctor will perform the operation in as little as sixty seconds. Officials are actually offered prizes for rounding up as many women as possible for the process. In 1992 almost 4 million women were sterilized this way.

Furthermore, in some countries, a man can commit acts such as battery, rape, and murder of a woman with little ramifications. In the Middle East, if a young girl is suspected of losing her virginity and staining her family's honor, she can be set on fire while she sleeps and officials often look the other way. In Pakistan, when a woman claims she was raped, she needs witnesses to attest to the crime along with four men to support her story. If she cannot prove her claim, she can be charged with adultery or with having tempted the rapist to commit the crime and will be severely punished. Since a woman's testimony is only worth half of a man's, one Pakistani woman says that "in cases of rape, men invariably get off free."[58] In the African country of Malawi, witch doctors tell men that if they have sex with a girl child they will become rich. The result of this is that young girls are raped repeatedly.

A weapon of war

Rape has been used as a weapon of war in Bosnia-Herzegovina, in ethnic warfare in Somalia, by Indian security forces in Kashmir, by both rebels and government forces in Peru, and under dictatorial rule in Haiti. The Bosnian Serbs recently created "rape camps" where women and girls were repeatedly raped until they became pregnant. They were then imprisoned for months so that they could not terminate the pregnancy. According to the Human Rights Watch Global Report on Women's Human Rights:

> Widely committed and seldom denounced, rape and sexual assault of women in situations of conflict have been viewed more as the spoils of war than as illegitimate acts that violate humanitarian law. Rape has long been mischaracterized and dismissed by military and political leaders—those in a position to stop it—as a private crime, a sexual act, the ignoble act of the occasional soldier; worse still, it has been accepted precisely because it is so commonplace.[59]

The international sex trade, which often includes forcing or tricking women into prostitution, is rampant across Asia.

A man in Thailand displays pictures of young girls who are available as prostitutes. Many of these girls have been sold into sexual slavery.

The sex trade in Thailand, for example, involves thousands of women and girls who were taken from their homes and sold into prostitution. Precedents for this behavior were set during World War II when Japan set up "comfort stations" and forced (at gunpoint) two hundred thousand Korean and native Japanese women as young as twelve years old to have sex with the soldiers on the front lines.

John Shattuck, the assistant secretary of state for Democracy, Human Rights, and Labor, fights for women's rights around the world. He believes that crimes against women should not go unpunished in the name of cultural tradition. He argues that violence and discrimination against women does not just victimize individuals; it holds back whole societies by confining the human potential of half the population. In the past few years, the United States has adopted the belief that women's rights are human rights and that everyone—regardless of their gender—deserves the same freedom and equality. The United Nations and the U.S. government are working to ensure that other countries will heed this message and will actively work towards improving the lives of women. By guaranteeing women their rights as human beings in society, that society is also making an investment in its future.

Notes

Introduction

1. Quoted in Sophie Yarborough, "Women Who Mean Business Give Each Other Support," *Long Beach Press-Telegram*, May 18, 1996.

Chapter 1: Women Fight for the Right to Vote: The Suffrage Movement

2. Mary Wollstonecraft, *A Vindication of the Rights of Woman*. New York: W. W. Norton, 1967.
3. Sarah M. Grimké, *Letters on the Equality of the Sexes and the Condition of Woman*. Boston: Isaac Knapp, 1838.
4. Quoted in Inez Hayes Irwin, *Angels and Amazons: A Hundred Years of American Women*. Garden City, NY: Doubleday, Doran, 1933.
5. Elizabeth Cady Stanton, *Eighty Years and More*. 1898. Reprint, Boston: Northeastern University Press, 1993.
6. Quoted in Janet Stevenson, *Women's Rights*. New York: Franklin Watts, 1972.
7. Quoted in Stevenson, *Women's Rights.*
8. Quoted in Lois Romano, "When Women Got the Vote: A Seventy-Fifth Anniversary Celebration," *Good Housekeeping*, March 1995.
9. Quoted in Romano, "When Women Got the Vote."

Chapter 2: Equality in Education

10. Quoted in Stevenson, *Women's Rights.*
11. Quoted in Stevenson, *Women's Rights.*
12. Quoted in David A. Kaplan, "VMI Braces for a Few Good Women," *Newsweek*, July 8, 1996.

13. Quoted in Elizabeth Gleick, "Let the Hell Week Begin," *Time*, August 26, 1996.
14. Quoted in Associated Press, "Woman Exposes Citadel Harassment," *San Mateo County Times*, February 15, 1997.
15. Quoted in Jackie Fitzpatrick, "Women's Lives, Women's Roles," *New York Times*, May 19, 1996.

Chapter 3: Equality in the Workplace

16. Quoted in Susan Gluck Mezey, *In Pursuit of Equality: Women, Public Policy, and the Federal Courts*. New York: St. Martin's Press, 1992.
17. Marcia D. Greenberger, testimony given before the U.S. House of Representatives Committee on Economic and Educational Opportunities, Subcommittee on Employer/Employee Relations, May 2, 1995.
18. Quoted in Ann Menache, "Women and Affirmative Action," *Independent Politics*, November/December 1995.
19. Ann Menache, "Women and Affirmative Action."
20. Quoted in A. E. Sadler, ed., *Affirmative Action*. San Diego: Greenhaven Press, 1996.
21. Quoted in "Excuse Me, Are Women Equal Yet?" *Glamour*, February 1996.
22. Mezey, *In Pursuit of Equality*.
23. Quoted in Mezey, *In Pursuit of Equality*.
24. Quoted in Sadler, *Affirmative Action*.
25. Michael Lynch and Katherine Post, "What Glass Ceiling?" *Public Interest*, Summer 1996.
26. Quoted in Elizabeth Larson, "No Thanks, Uncle Sam," *Freeman*, December 1995.
27. Quoted in "Excuse Me, Are Women Equal Yet?"
28. Quoted in Amy Saltzman, "Life After the Lawsuit," *U.S. News & World Report*, August 19, 1996.
29. Barbara F. Reskin and Irene Padavic, *Women and Men at Work*. Thousand Oaks, CA: Pine Forge Press, 1994.
30. Quoted in Susan Deller Ross et al., *The Rights of Women—Basic ACLU Guide to Women's Rights*. 3rd ed. Carbondale: Southern Illinois University Press, 1993.

31. Quoted in Deborah L. Jacobs, "Back from the Mommy Track," *New York Times*, October 9, 1994.
32. Quoted in Leslie Kaufman, "A Report from the Front: Why It Has Gotten Easier to Sue for Sexual Harassment," *Newsweek*, January 13, 1997.
33. Quoted in Leslie Alderman, "Stand Up for Your Rights on the Job," *Money*, March 1997.
34. Quoted in Tamar Stieber, "The Nuts and Sluts Strategy," *Glamour*, August 1996.

Chapter 4: Violence Against Women

35. Quoted in Ruth Shalit, "Caught in the Act," *New Republic*, July 12, 1993.
36. Quoted in Andrea Rock, "Unequal Justice," *Ladies Home Journal*, April 1995.
37. Report from Maryland Special Joint Committee on Gender Bias in the Courts, 1989.
38. Quoted in David Gelmen et al., "The Mind of the Rapist," *Newsweek*, July 23, 1990.
39. Quoted in Rock, "Unequal Justice."
40. National Organization for Women, *Together We Can Stop the Violence* (brochure), Washington, DC, n.d.

Chapter 5: Reproductive Rights

41. Quoted in Lawrence Lader and Milton Meltzer, *Margaret Sanger: Pioneer of Birth Control.* New York: Thomas Y. Crowell, 1969.
42. Quoted in Lader and Meltzer, *Margaret Sanger.*
43. Quoted in Lauran Neergaard, "FDA Approves the Morning After Pill," *Associated Press Wire*, February 24, 1997.
44. Quoted in Mezey, *In Pursuit of Equality.*
45. Quoted in Mezey, *In Pursuit of Equality.*
46. Linda Greenhouse, "High Court Upholds Buffer Zone of 15 Feet at Abortion Clinics," *New York Times*, February 20, 1997.

47. Quoted in Greenhouse, "High Court Upholds Buffer Zone."

Chapter 6: The Plight of Women Around the Globe

48. Hillary Rodham Clinton, "Women's Rights Are Human Rights," *Vital Speeches of the Day*, October 1, 1995.
49. Tracy Rubin, "Human Rights Are Women's Rights, Women's Rights Are Human Rights," *Knight-Ridder/Tribune News Service*, September 13, 1995.
50. Quoted in Rod Nordland, "The Islamic Nightmare," *Newsweek*, October 14, 1996.
51. Quoted in "Feminism Reaches Japan," *Economist*, June 1, 1996.
52. Quoted in Katherine E. Young, "Loyal Wives, Virtuous Mothers," *Russian Life*, March 1996.
53. Quoted in Young, "Loyal Wives, Virtuous Mothers."
54. Quoted in Rupert J. Taylor, "Mosadi: Abuse Against Women Around the World," *Canada and the World Backgrounder*, January 1995.
55. Quoted in Allison Bell, "Worldwide Women's Watch," *Teen*, June 1996.
56. Quoted in Bell, "Worldwide Women's Watch."
57. Quoted in Bell, "Worldwide Women's Watch."
58. Quoted in Taylor, "Mosadi."
59. Quoted in Leslie Wirpsa, "New Study Documents Abuses of Women's Rights Worldwide," *National Catholic Reporter*, September 29, 1995.

Organizations to Contact

Equal Employment Opportunity Commission (EEOC)
1801 L St. NW
Washington, DC 20507
(202) 663-4900

The EEOC investigates and prosecutes cases of sexual discrimination and harassment. It also offers educational information for employers and community organizations.

National Abortion Federation
1426 U St. NW, Suite 103
Washington, DC 20009
(202) 667-5881

The federation supplies information on current abortion laws and practices and offers a free fact sheet, *Teenage Women, Abortion, and the Law.*

National Coalition Against Domestic Violence
PO Box 18749
Denver, CO 80218-0749
(303) 839-1852

The coalition works to end domestic violence and to support its victims. It maintains a nationwide directory of battered women's shelters and hotlines including a breakdown of the kinds of services each provides.

National Domestic Violence Hotline
(800) 799-SAFE (7233)
TDD number for hearing impaired: (800) 787-3224

This toll-free crisis hotline will provide callers with crisis intervention, counseling, and information about their rights regarding domestic violence. It will also connect a caller to his or her local police station in case of emergency.

National Organization for Women (NOW)
1000 16th St. NW, Suite 700
Washington, DC 20036
(202) 331-0066

NOW is the largest women's rights organization in the country, with local chapters in over six hundred cities. It offers educational information on current issues and related legislation and encourages individual involvement at the community level.

National Women's Political Caucus
1275 K St. NW, Suite 750
Washington, DC 20005
(202) 785-1100

The caucus supplies information and newsletters to voters on current women's issues and upcoming political debate. Through its databases of phone numbers of politicians in each state, it can direct the interested person to appropriate legislators and local chapters concerned with securing women's rights.

Progressive Resources Catalogue
Donnelly/Colt
Box 188
Hampton, CT 06247
(203) 455-9621

A catalog full of creative, innovative, and inexpensive ways to express one's position on women's and human rights. One popular item is the "This Insults Women" sticker that the consumer can stick on an offensive advertisement or other public display.

Rape Abuse Incest National Network (RAINN)
(800) 656-HOPE (4673)

A toll-free crisis hotline set up by singer Tori Amos and Atlantic records that will direct the caller to the nearest crisis center for immediate help from a counselor.

Suggestions for Further Reading

Dale Carlson, *Girls Are Equal Too: The Women's Movement for Teenagers*. New York: Atheneum, 1973. Though written in 1973, much of this book applies today. It offers great explanations of why women and girls have historically had a second-class position in society. It also looks into the negative stereotypes of women that society and the media foster.

Donna Jackson, *How to Make the World a Better Place for Women in Five Minutes a Day.* New York: Hyperion, 1992. Filled with fascinating facts and suggestions for action, this terrific handbook is complete with phone numbers and addresses so readers inspired by something in the book will know exactly how to reach that organization to get involved, or where to buy a certain product that benefits women. A "must have" for anyone concerned with the rights of women and girls today.

Lawrence Lader and Milton Meltzer, *Margaret Sanger: Pioneer of Birth Control.* New York: Thomas Y. Crowell, 1969. An easy-to-read biography about a truly remarkable woman. The book traces Margaret Sanger's life from childhood until her death, bringing her to life for the reader. Her struggle to get birth control accepted in America is detailed along with her personal triumphs and tragedies.

Miriam Sagan, *Women's Suffrage.* San Diego: Lucent Books, 1996. A very thorough look at the women's rights movement at the time of the campaign for suffrage. It includes a timeline for easy understanding of the events, and discusses the major issues of the day in a clear and straightforward manner.

Janet Stevenson, *Women's Rights*. New York: Franklin Watts, 1972. Traces the history of the early women's rights movement in the United States, with brief profiles of the women who led it. It serves as a great foundation for the reader who wants to learn about what life was like in the eighteenth and early nineteenth centuries.

Susan Strauss, *Sexual Harassment and Teens: A Program for Positive Change.* Minneapolis: Free Spirit Publishing, 1992. This comprehensive program helps teens understand the causes and consequences of sexual harassment. It is designed for grades seven to twelve and includes forty reproducible forms, handouts, and surveys so that schools, community organizations, and youth groups can follow the program as a group.

George Sullivan, *The Day the Women Got the Vote*. New York: Scholastic, 1994. Describes not only the fight for the vote, but all the other battles women are fighting for—equality in the workplace, in the home, in society in general. Filled with rare black-and-white photographs that really give the reader a feel for the period.

Mandy Wharton, *Rights of Women*. New York: Gloucester Press, 1989. A broad look at women's roles in American life and around the world. Filled with colorful pictures depicting the different parts of a woman's life.

Works Consulted

Leslie Alderman, "Stand Up for Your Rights on the Job," *Money*, March 1997.

Associated Press, "Woman Exposes Citadel Harassment," *San Mateo County Times*, February 15, 1997.

Allison Bell, "Worldwide Women's Watch," *Teen*, June 1996.

Hillary Rodham Clinton, "Women's Rights Are Human Rights," *Vital Speeches of the Day*, October 1, 1995.

"Excuse Me, Are Women Equal Yet?" *Glamour*, February 1996.

"Feminism Reaches Japan," *Economist*, June 1, 1996

Jackie Fitzpatrick, "Women's Lives, Women's Roles," *New York Times*, May 19, 1996.

David Gelmen et al, "The Mind of the Rapist," *Newsweek*, July 23, 1990.

Elizabeth Gleick, "Let the Hell Week Begin," *Time*, August 26, 1996.

Marcia D. Greenberger, testimony given before the U.S. House of Representatives Committee on Economic and Educational Opportunities, Subcommittee on Employer/Employee Relations, May 2, 1995.

Linda Greenhouse, "High Court Upholds Buffer Zone of 15 Feet at Abortion Clinics," *New York Times*, February 20, 1997.

Sarah M. Grimké, *Letters on the Equality of the Sexes and the Condition of Woman*. Boston: Isaac Knapp, 1838.

Inez Hayes Irwin, *Angels and Amazons: A Hundred Years of American Women*. Garden City, NY: Doubleday, Doran, 1933.

Deborah L. Jacobs, "Back from the Mommy Track," *New York Times*, October 9, 1994.

David A. Kaplan, "*VMI Braces for a Few Good Women*," *Newsweek*, July 8, 1996.

Leslie Kaufman, "A Report from the Front: Why It Has Gotten Easier to Sue for Sexual Harassment," *Newsweek*, January 13, 1997.

Elizabeth Larson, "No Thanks, Uncle Sam," *Freeman*, December 1995.

Michael Lynch and Katherine Post, "What Glass Ceiling?" *Public Interest*, Summer 1996.

Wilfred M. McClay, "Of 'Rats' and Women," *Commentary*, September 1996.

Ann Menache, "Women and Affirmative Action," *Independent Politics*, November/December 1995.

Susan Gluck Mezey, *In Pursuit of Equality: Women, Public Policy, and the Federal Courts*. New York: St. Martin's Press, 1992.

National Organization for Women, *Together We Can Stop the Violence* (brochure), Washington, DC, n.d.

Lauran Neergaard, "FDA Approves the Morning After Pill," *Associated Press Wire*, February 24, 1997.

Rod Nordland, "The Islamic Nightmare," *Newsweek*, October 14, 1996.

Report from Maryland Special Joint Committee on Gender Bias in the Courts, 1989.

Barbara F. Reskin and Irene Padavic, *Women and Men at Work*. Thousand Oaks, CA: Pine Forge Press, 1994.

Andrea Rock, "Unequal Justice," *Ladies Home Journal*, April 1995.

Lois Romano, "When Women Got the Vote: A Seventy-Fifth Anniversary Celebration," *Good Housekeeping*, March 1995.

Susan Deller Ross et al., *The Rights of Women—Basic ACLU Guide to Women's Rights*. 3rd ed. Carbondale: Southern Illinois University Press, 1993.

Tracy Rubin, "Human Rights Are Women's Rights, Women's Rights Are Human Rights," *Knight-Ridder/Tribune News Service*, September 13, 1995.

A. E. Sadler, ed., *Affirmative Action*. San Diego: Greenhaven Press, 1996.

Amy Saltzman, "Life After the Lawsuit," *U.S. News & World Report*, August 19, 1996.

Ruth Shalit, "Caught in the Act," *New Republic*, July 12, 1993.

Elizabeth Cady Stanton, *Eighty Years and More*. 1898. Reprint, Boston: Northeastern University Press, 1993.

Janet Stevenson, *Women's Rights*. New York: Franklin Watts, 1972.

Karin L. Swisher, ed., *Violence Against Women*. San Diego: Greenhaven Press, 1994.

Rupert J. Taylor, "Mosadi: Abuse Against Women Around the World," *Canada and the World Backgrounder*, January 1995.

Leslie Wirpsa, "New Study Documents Abuses of Women's Rights Worldwide," *National Catholic Reporter*, September 29, 1995.

Mary Wollstonecraft, *A Vindication of the Rights of Woman*. New York: W. W. Norton, 1967.

Sophie Yarborough, "Women Who Mean Business Give Each Other Support," *Long Beach Press-Telegram*, May 18, 1996.

Katherine E. Young, "Loyal Wives, Virtuous Mothers," *Russian Life*, March 1996.

Index

abolitionist movement, 10–11, 13
abortion
  clinics, 66–67
  constitutional right to, 62–63
  illegal, 63
  in Ireland, 74–75
  minors and, 66
  Pill, the, and, 62
  protesters against, 66–67
  restrictions on
    federal, 63–64
    state, 64–66
  RU486 and, 61–62
  in Russia, 75
  violence against providers, 67–68
Abortion Control Act, 65
Advocates for Life Ministries, 68
affirmative action
  California ban of, 35
  defense of, 34–35, 36
  definition of, 33–34
  opposition to, 34
Afghanistan
  education in, 71
  employment in, 73–74
Algeria, 74
All Women's Health Services, 68
American Anti-Slavery Society, 10
American Birth Control League, 60
American Medical Association, 60
American Woman Suffrage
  Association, 13
Anthony, Susan B., 12
  motto of, 17
  National Woman Suffrage
    Association and, 13
  wording of Nineteenth Amendment
    and, 15
Asia, 78–79
athletics, 20, 21

battered women's shelters, 49–50
Bell, Becky, 66
Bethune, Mary McLeod, 30–31
Biden, Joseph
  on Violence Against Women Act, 47
  on women victims of violence, 48
birth control, 6
  access to, 59–60
  in China, 75
  in India, 75, 77–78
  in Japan, 75
  opponents of, 62
  Pill, the, and, 61, 62
  in Rumania, 75
  in Russia, 75
  sterilization and, 77–78
bona fide occupational qualification
  (BFOQ), 32–33
Bosnia-Herzegovina, 78
Brennan, William, 63–64
Bryn Mawr College, 20

California
  affirmative action and, 35
  domestic violence legislation in, 53
  education and, 22
  sexual harassment in, 45
Catt, Carrie Chapman, 15, 16
children
  effect of increase in women's
    employment on, 26, 28, 40, 41–43
  in garment industry, 28–29
  violence and, 50, 51
China
  birth control in, 75
  employment in, 72
  female infanticide in, 77
  UN Fourth World Conference on
    Women, 69
Citadel
  first coeducational class at, 24–25
  sexual harassment at, 25–26
  Shannon Faulkner and, 22–23
Civil Rights Act (1964), 22, 27, 32,
  33, 44
Civil Rights Restoration Act, 21
Clinton, Bill, 43, 47
  Family Medical Leave Act and,
    41–42

Freedom of Access to Clinics Act and, 67
National Domestic Violence Hotline and, 51
Coalition Against Domestic Violence, 54
colleges
rape in, 56–57
women and, 20
Community Policing to Combat Domestic Violence, 49
Comstock laws, 60
Congressional Union for Woman Suffrage, 15
contraceptives. *See* birth control

Declaration of Independence, 6
Declaration of Sentiments and Resolutions, 11–12
domestic violence, 46
hospitals and, 54
hotlines, 51
mandatory arrest and, 54
mandatory reporting and, 54
prosecution of, 51, 52–53, 57
state legislation, 53
worldwide, 77
Douglass, Frederick, 12
dowries, 76–77

education
in Afghanistan, 71
discrimination in, 20, 22–23, 26
in 1800s, 9, 18
faculties, women on, 26–27, 38–39
federal role in, 20–22
in Japan, 70–71
worldwide, 70
Educational Amendments Act, 20, 21, 27
Education Task Force, 21
Egypt, 76
employment
advancement in, 39–41
in Afghanistan, 73–74
in China, 72
discrimination
in education, 26
in industry, 30, 31, 32
in Japan, 71–72
quotas, 33–34
in Russia, 72–73
in schools, 26–27, 38–39
state legislation, 33
in United States, 28–29, 30, 31

Equal Educational Opportunities Act, 22
Equal Employment Opportunity Act, 32
Equal Pay Act (EPA), 27, 36–37
Equal Protection Clause, 27
Equal Rights Amendment (ERA), 7
Executive Order 11246, 33

Family and Medical Leave Act (FMLA), 41–42
family planning. *See* birth control
Faulkner, Shannon, 22–23
Feinstein, Dianne, 16–17
female genital mutilation (FGM), 75–76
female infanticide, 77
Freedom of Access to Clinics Act, 67
Friedan, Betty, 6–7
Full Faith and Credit provision, 55–56

garment industry, 28–29
glass ceiling, 39–41
Grimké, Angelina, 10–11
Grimké, Sarah, 10–11
Griswold v. Connecticut, 61

Haiti, 78
Harvard University, 20, 26, 27
Haynes, Audrey Tayse, 35–36
health care, 74
homelessness, 50
hotlines, 51
Human Rights Watch
on dowries in India, 77
on rape, 78
on status of women in India, 75
Hyde Amendment (1976), 63

illiteracy, 70
India
birth control in, 75, 77–78
domestic violence in, 77
dowries and, 77
female infanticide in, 77
marriage in, 76–77
rape and, 78
women's status in, 75
Iran, 77
Ireland, 74–75

Jacob Wetterling Act, 47, 57–58
Japan
birth control in, 75
comfort stations in, 79
education in, 70–71

employment in, 71–72

Kennedy, John F., 33, 36

law enforcement training, 48
League of Women Voters, 16
liquor industry, 14
Lord Hale instructions, 55

Malawi, 78
marriage, 76–77
maternity leave, 42–43
maternity-related deaths, 74
Medicaid, 63
Mill, John Stuart, 9–10
Mitsubishi Motor Manufacturing of America, 45
Mother of the Suffrage Movement. *See* Stanton, Elizabeth Cady
Mott, Lucretia, 10, 11, 12

National American Woman Suffrage Association, 15
National Birth Control League, 60
National Organization for Women (NOW), 7, 58
National Woman Suffrage Association, 13
National Women's Party, 15
Nigeria, 76

Pakistan, 78
Paul, Alice, 15
Perkins, Frances, 30–31
Peru, 78
Philadephia Female Anti-Slavery Society, 10
Pill, the, 61, 62
Planned Parenthood Federation, 60, 64–65
poverty, feminization of, 71
Pregnancy Discrimination Act, 41
prostitution, 78–79
protection, orders of, 54–55

quotas, employment, 33–34

rape, 46
  in college, 56–57
  previous convictions of, 55–56
  prosecution of, 51–53, 57
  as weapon of war, 78
Rape Abuse Incest National Network (RAINN), 51
Rape Shields, 55
right of privacy, 61
Roe v. Wade, 62–64
Roosevelt, Eleanor, 30, 36
RU486, 61–62
Rumania, 75
Rush, Benjamin, 18–19
Russia
  abortion and, 75
  birth control in, 75
  employment in, 72–73
  maternity-related deaths in, 74

salaries
  in 1800s, 8
  in garment industry, 28–29
  inequality between men's and women's, 30, 36–38
  market demand and, 37
  during World War I, 30
Sanger, Margaret, 59–60
Saudi Arabia, 73
Scalia, Antonin, 23
Schafran, Lynn Hecht
  on sentencing rapists, 52–53
  on sexual harassment cases, 45
Seneca Falls, N.Y., 11–12
sex offenders, 57–58
sex trade, 78–79
sexual assault. *See* rape
sexual harassment
  in college, 25–26
  cost to companies, 44–45
  court cases, 44, 45
  in employment, 43–44
Somalia, 76, 78
South Carolina, 22–23, 24–26
Stanton, Elizabeth Cady, 19
  abolitionist movement and, 11, 13
  on equality of men and women, 11–12
  on importance of women's rights, 6
  on reaction to suffrage movement, 12
statistical discrimination, 41
status of women, in 1800s, 8–9, 18, 20
Steinem, Gloria, 7
sterilization, 77–78
Stone, Lucy, 12, 13
STOP, 48–49
Student Right to Know and Campus Security Act, 56–57
Subjection of Women, The (Mill), 9–10
suffrage movement
  abolitionist movement and, 10–11, 13
  beginnings of, 7, 9–10

in Colorado, 15
effects of, 15, 16–17
in Idaho, 15
opponents of, 14
reaction to, 12
split in, 13, 15
temperance movement and, 14
in Utah, 15
in Wyoming, 14–15
sweatshops, 29
Syria, 77

Take Back the Night, 58
Taliban, 71, 73
temperance movement, 13–14
Thailand, 79
Thomas, Clarence, 23, 43
Title IV (Civil Rights Act of 1964), 22, 27
Title VII (Civil Rights Act of 1964), 27, 32, 33, 44
Title IX (Educational Amendments Act), 20, 21, 27
Troy Female Seminary, 19

United Nations, 69
United States
Civil Rights Commission, 38
Civil War, 12–13
Commission on the Status of Women, 36–37
Constitution
Eighteenth Amendment, 15
Fourteenth Amendment, 13
Nineteenth Amendment, 15–16
Thirteenth Amendment, 13
Equal Employment Opportunity Commission (EEOC), 40–41
equal pay and, 37
sexual harassment and, 43–44
female genital mutilation and, 76
Food and Drug Administration (FDA), 61–62
legislation. *See specific acts*
National Domestic Violence Hotline, 51
role in education, 20–22
Supreme Court
abortion and, 62–66, 67
birth control and, 61
education and, 21, 23, 27

Vindication of the Rights of Women, A, (Wollstonecraft), 9
violence against women
incidence of, 46
prevention of, 50–51
prosecution of, 51–53, 57
state legislation on, 48, 53
see also domestic violence; rape
Violence Against Women Act (VAWA)
battered women's shelters and, 49–50
Full Faith and Credit provision, 55–56
Jacob Wetterling Act, 47, 57–58
orders of protection and, 55
provisions of, 46–47
repeat offenders and, 53
STOP funds, 48–49
Violent Crime Control and Law Enforcement Act. *See* Violence Against Women Act (VAWA)
Virginia, 22, 23–24, 26
Virginia Military Institute (VMI), 22, 23–24, 26

Wal-Mart, 44–45
Webster v. Reproductive Health Services, 64–65
Williams v. Saxbe, 44
Wollstonecraft, Mary, 9
Woman's Christian Temperance Union, 14
Women's Equity Action League, 26
Women's National Loyalty League, 13
Women's Rights and the Law, 33
Women's Rights Convention (1848), 11–12
working mothers, 26, 28, 40, 41–43
World Anti-Slavery Convention, 11
World War I, 29–30
World War II, 31

About the Author

Wendy Mass holds a B.A. in English from Tufts University and an M.A. in Creative Writing from California State University, Long Beach. She is the cofounder and editor of a national literary journal for teenagers called *Writes of Passage* and is the author of fiction and nonfiction books and articles for young adults. She has worked as a book editor for Longmeadow Press and Reader's Digest Young Families and currently lives in San Francisco, California.

Picture Credits

Cover photo: Catherine Smith/Impact Visuals
Bill Burke, Impact Visuals, 42
David Bacon, Impact Visuals, 36
J. K. Condyles, Impact Visuals, 55, 76
Corbis-Bettmann, 9
Dictionary of American Portraits, Dover Publications, 11
FDR Library, 30
Harvey Finkle, Impact Visuals, 64
Jerome Friar, Impact Visuals, 65
P. Hasegawa, Impact Visuals, 72
Carolina Kroon, Impact Visuals, 58
Jack Kurtz, Impact Visuals, 49, 56
Library of Congress, 7, 10, 12, 14, 15, 16, 19, 61
Steve Latimer, Impact Visuals, 47
National Archives, 31
Heldur Netocny, Impact Visuals, 79
Reuters/Corbis Bettmann, 24
Reuters/Ira Schwarz/Archive Photos, 62
Reuters/Jason Reed/Archive Photos, 70
Trades and Occupations, Dover Publications, 29
Teun Voeten, Impact Visuals, 74
UPI/Corbis-Bettmann, 67, 68